CONNECT

CONNECT

an exposition of Psalm 1
how to meditate biblically

Rob Dingman

LINE
UPON
LINE

Connect
an exposition of Psalm 1
how to meditate biblically

© 2022 Rob Dingman
All rights reserved.
Published 2022

ISBN 978-0-9571329-5-5

Published by Line Upon Line
www.calvarytw.uk

Designed by Hand-Maid Design, London
Set in Adobe Chapparal Pro
Chapter heads and subheads in Museo Sans 700

To Joanie, Holly, André, Katie,
my family whom I love.

For with God nothing will be impossible.
Luke 1:37

The LORD will perfect that which concerns me;
Your mercy, O LORD, endures forever;
Do not forsake the works of Your hands.
Psalm 138:8

Contents

Preface

My morning time is absolutely delicious.

That's the best way to describe what it's like for me to be with the God who lives forever. I get to taste Someone infinitely interesting and vital. He is significant, and when He touches me, I become significant too; He influences me, and I in turn influence others. Am I anyone important? No, but He sure is.

The point is, God wants this deliciousness for you as well.

I call the book *Connect* because when you meditate on the Word of God, you connect with Him. You'll see this link is real like a root—not a piece of self-hypnosis, but vital so that your life will be transformed.

When you receive the benefit from this, you'll be able to pass it on to someone else. Your life will impact those in your orbit. You are really going to enjoy that.

Bless you today,
Rob Dingman
Pastor, Calvary Chapel Twickenham
London, England

CONNECT

Part 1 • Exposition of Psalm 1

Blessed is the man who walks not in the counsel of the ungodly, nor stands in the path of sinners, nor sits in the seat of the scornful;

But his delight is in the law of the LORD, and in His law he meditates day and night.

He shall be like a tree planted by the rivers of water, that brings forth its fruit in its season, whose leaf also shall not wither; and whatever he does shall prosper.

The ungodly are not so, but are like the chaff which the wind drives away.

Therefore the ungodly shall not stand in the judgment, nor sinners in the congregation of the righteous.

For the LORD knows the way of the righteous, but the way of the ungodly shall perish.

Psalm 1:1 Blessed is the man
Who walks not in the counsel of the ungodly,
Nor stands in the path of sinners,
Nor sits in the seat of the scornful.

1

Blessing Is All,
or Nothing at All

PSALM 1 DECLARES, "Blessed." The psalmist sees two paths men use to approach blessedness. Only one of them works. The other path leads to the opposite condition, which we will consider in due course.

Blessed. What does it mean, and why is it all-important?

In Hebrew, the original language, blessed means "happy." This is not subjective happiness. If it were, happiness would be a matter of taste. What makes you happy doesn't necessarily make me happy. There's no right or wrong answer. Psalm 1 is about ultimate happiness—complete, total, and transcendent—so that translators always use the word *blessed* in Psalm 1:1.

What's the difference?

One difference is in their etymologies. The word *happy* contains the Anglo-Saxon particle "hap," referring to chance and external circumstances. It shows up in "happen," "mayhap," and "happenstance." For example, "Luck, chance—it all came together. I won the lottery, and now I'm happy." If I don't like what is happening, I'm not happy. The English word *happiness* is all about impersonal chance and all about me.

In contrast, *bless* comes from an Old English word meaning "blood". In the Bible, the blood of a perfect sacrifice was used to purify people and things from all defilement to become God's possession. *Holy* means sacred, pure, clean, for His purpose and His glory.

There's a big difference between my purpose—aiming for my happiness—and God's purpose—making me holy for Himself.

Another difference is in permanence

Happiness won't happen automatically. If I work hard, take advantage of opportunities, and make the breaks, maybe I can get what I want. But despite all my hard work, things happen outside my control that affect my happiness. Things like industrial actions, government regulations, wars, storms, earthquakes, fires, tsunamis, power outages, delays, economic turndowns, stock market crashes, terrorist attacks, broadband slowdown, and death. I might be in the wrong place at the wrong time. There's nothing I can do about that.

God steers His blessing. He's got His eye on His people. He won't leave them until He blesses them.

I know this because while reading 2 Timothy one day, I noticed this:

[God] has saved us and called us with a holy calling, not according to our works, but according to His own purpose and grace which was given to us in Christ Jesus before time began. (2 Timothy 1:9)

God gave us purpose and grace in Christ Jesus before time began. That means His purpose and grace are eternal. God has always determined to bless us with salvation and not destroy us like we deserve. The devil fights God's purpose with all his schemes and might. He wants to derail grace and destroy salvation. Will he succeed? Second Timothy 1:9 shows that he can't because he's not eternal. His temporary purpose is limited by his finite power. At a certain point, his allotted time will run out. His power and freedom to act will come to an end. But God's eternal purpose and grace cannot be changed or nullified by any temporary thing that opposes Him. Therefore, blessing is permanent and certain.

Notice how many bad things happen to God's people in the Bible

Abraham's wife Sarah was barren. So were Rebekah and Rachel, the wives of Isaac and Jacob. Manoah's wife was barren. Hannah and Elizabeth were also barren.

Jacob was cheated over and over by his father-in-law.

Joseph was hated by his brothers, sold into slavery, slandered, imprisoned, and forgotten.

David was attacked and hated by Saul—and by his own son, Absalom.

Job was oppressed by Satan, who was permitted by God to do so.

Zerubbabel was overwhelmed by the enormity of his task to rebuild the Temple.

John the Baptist was imprisoned and beheaded.

Paul was shipwrecked, in dangers, hungry, cold, exhausted, and fearful.

After twenty barren years, Rebekah conceived and then had a difficult pregnancy. She asked what we all would have asked: "If all is well, why am I like this?" (Genesis 25:22).

God's people do not live in a hermetically sealed glasshouse with only good things happening to them. They go through terrible things that seem random and purposeless.

But we see throughout the Bible that the Lord causes all things to "work together for good to those who love God, to those who are the called according to His purpose" (Romans 8:28). Paul says we know this to be a fact.

"Happy" is pitiful. Random forces without a definite aim, rule, or method have to hit your jackpot, for a limited time.

God works out His eternal plan for you with all knowledge and power. All the opposition is temporary, limited, and weak; therefore, nothing can stop Him.

Blessing is different from happiness in its scope

Happiness is about me alone. If I attain happiness, that's what matters. I just want to be happy. Blessing is about me, but it doesn't stop with just me. God blessing me is a prelude to blessing the world, which He revealed when He blessed Abram:

Now the LORD had said to Abram:
"Get out of your country,
From your family
And from your father's house,
To a land that I will show you.
I will make you a great nation;
I will bless you
And make your name great;
And you shall be a blessing.
I will bless those who bless you,
And I will curse him who curses you;
And in you all the families of the earth shall be blessed."
(Genesis 12:1–3)

Yes, God was concerned to bless Abraham, and He began with Isaac, the child of promise. That child led to the creation of God's chosen people, the Jews. Through them came the written words of God—the Law, the Prophets, and the Psalms. Through the people and the Scriptures came Jesus, the Messiah, to fulfill eternal salvation by His crucifixion and resurrection. Jesus poured forth His Holy Spirit upon the church to bring the good news to the world. The culmination of salvation, says Paul in Romans 11:15, will be the restoration of Israel and life from the dead. God's blessing always goes beyond personal blessing.

David learned that his sufferings were actually God's blessing so that others would also be blessed:

I waited patiently for the LORD;
And He inclined to me,

And heard my cry.
He also brought me up out of a horrible pit,
Out of the miry clay,
And set my feet upon a rock,
And established my steps.
He has put a new song in my mouth—
Praise to our God;
Many will see it and fear,
And will trust in the LORD. (Psalm 40:1–3)

God had more in view than David's relief from a horrible pit. He saved David so that others watching would know God could save them too. David inspired future generations to rely on God. God created us to be significant—to bless us and through us to bless others. That's why Jesus said, "It is more blessed to give than to receive" (Acts 20:35).

It helps to define a thing by its opposite

The opposite of blessing is cursing. Cursing is the power of God to oppose, harm, make bad, or destroy. People can bless and curse as well, and they have some power to make it happen. God holds all the power of cursing. What He curses cannot be remedied.

When God blesses you, it's always for good, to hear and answer your prayer and do good for you in the end. Hannah prayed for God to remember her, and He listened and gave her a son (1 Samuel 1).

When God curses you, He doesn't bless, He doesn't hear prayer, He doesn't regard who you are. He pays no attention to you. He forgets you.

Consider the lake of fire, the last judgment found in Revelation 20. Everyone and everything cast into that fire will never come out. That's the opposite of blessing.

Is there any state in between blessing and cursing? Think about it.

God wants the best. The devil wants the worst. Blessing is binary; it's a matter of eternal life or eternal death. It's all or nothing at all.

You want to be definitely, certainly, and eternally blessed by God. You don't want to be temporarily happy as a result of time and chance and your hard work. You certainly don't want to be cursed. Anything less than eternal life is a stay of execution.

What are the things that make for blessing? That's the subject of my next chapter.

Psalm 1:1 Blessed is the man
Who walks not in the counsel of the ungodly,
Nor stands in the path of sinners,
Nor sits in the seat of the scornful.

2

The Wrong Way,
or
I Know Exactly What
I'm Doing!

BLESSING BEGINS BY not doing something, or better, by changing our course of action. That is, we stop going in the way of the ungodly.

The psalmist contrasts two opposing ways, those of the ungodly man and the blessed man.

The blessed man delights in the law of God and meditates in it day and night. He submits to all it reveals and demands, and he finds it reasonable to do so. He wants to do the will of God.

The ungodly man acts the opposite way toward the Word of God: he hates it, ignores it, and rejects it. He is on his own path, seeking his own will and happiness.

What is so bad about doing my own thing and not God's thing? The paths are mutually exclusive. You can't go God's way and your own way at the same time. If you do what God wants, you can't do what you want. That's what the apostle Paul says in Galatians 5:16–17: "I say then: Walk in the Spirit, and you shall not fulfill the lust of the flesh. For the flesh lusts against the Spirit, and the Spirit against the flesh; and these are contrary to one another, so that you do not do the things that you wish."

Leave God, leave life

The first evil is leaving God, the fountain of living waters, where life itself comes from. When a people leave their relationship with the Lord, they leave life.

> **"For pass beyond the coasts of Cyprus and see,**
> **Send to Kedar and consider diligently,**
> **And see if there has been such a thing.**
> **Has a nation changed its gods,**
> **Which are not gods?**
> **But My people have changed their Glory**
> **For what does not profit.**
> **Be astonished, O heavens, at this,**
> **And be horribly afraid;**
> **Be very desolate," says the LORD.**
> **"For My people have committed two evils:**
> **They have forsaken Me, the fountain of living waters,**

And hewn themselves cisterns—broken cisterns that can hold no water." (Jeremiah 2:10–13)

The second evil is thinking nothing is going to happen when we leave the fountain. We're not stupid! We know we need water. But we have our own supply! We're going to be fine!

God says, look at your buckets. They only hold so much water. And worse, they leak. Everything in this world is temporary, finite, and futile. You are going to run out of life. Then what will you do?

Don't worry! The ungodly have counsel, tips, and lifehacks to help you find life. They encourage and exhort the world to pursue almost anything to find life: intellectual and fleshly pursuits, indulgent and ascetic pursuits, religious and secular pursuits, big goals and small goals. So what if these methods contradict each other? They are all consistent with the big goal. Pursue anything but God in order to find life.

In the end, every attempt to pursue life suffers a mortal flaw. It doesn't give to you, it takes from you. The bucket leaks and you are exhausted. You continue existing without being satisfied.

In 2013 I visited the Democratic Republic of Congo to teach a pastors conference. My host pointed out the roadside vendors standing next to their pathetic, odd assortments of little things to sell. I was told that these people only ate when they sold something. They might go two or three days without a sale so they have to live hungry. Imagine you must dig a ditch in the hot sun, perspiring your brains out with no way to get a drink. Being forced to exist without satisfaction is the very definition of misery.

We are more than just physical beings with bodily appetites. Feeding our bodies does not feed our souls.

Our needs must be satisfied by the right input

Wouldn't it be great if cars ran on sugar water? It would be a lot cheaper than gasoline or diesel. But cars can only burn one fuel. If you have ever put petrol in your diesel car, you've learned the awful truth: there is no substitute for the one fuel your car was designed to use.

God designed the human body. It has operating specifications we can't ignore without wrecking ourselves. Our bodies run on sugar! The simplest carbohydrate, glucose, is our fuel. Without glucose, we starve. Roughage is good for us, but it is no substitute for carbohydrate.

God made the human soul to live in the body, and it also has operating specifications. God says man does not live by bread alone. Our minds are designed to operate on 100% truth. If we live by 99% truth and 1% lie, that lie will betray and destroy us.

Our hearts were designed to operate on 100% divine love. God's love esteems the one He loves as more important than Himself. He "so loved the world that He gave His only begotten Son, that whoever believes in Him should not perish but have everlasting life" (John 3:16). There is no greater love. Any substitute love is self-serving and will only abuse, deceive, and betray us.

Are you miserable? Do you need life?

Without God we are like those roadside vendors in Congo, only worse. They might make a sale. With us, there is no sale to expect. We can only exist in misery as we grope in the dark for truth and love.

We're all in the same desperate fix. We need life.

Only Jesus rose from the dead. Only He gives eternal life. All the other solutions people offer are subtle variations of death.

Therefore, we cannot accept the counsel of those who have left God.

Who has authority to give peace?

When we go away from God, we forsake life. We also set ourselves up as authorities in place of God.

This is an obvious corollary. If we reject and discard God, then there is no being higher than us. Humans are now the boss, and humans determine what is right and what is wrong.

Now we have a problem of authority. Why should I obey you, Mr. Sir? Why don't you obey me? Who is the standard? Who is the measuring rod? Who is to say that I'm wrong? Without an absolute standard, we open the door to absolute confusion. Chaos can only be resisted by imposing order by force. A quote attributed to Mao Zedong states, "Political power grows out of the barrel of a gun."[1]

We certainly absolve one another of wrongdoing. A priest can hear a confession and say a person is forgiven. A psychologist can help someone make better choices and think in a more integrated way. But who has the authority to bestow peace?

As a Boy Scout, I had to pass certain outdoor cooking requirements to earn advancement. On one camping trip we were required to cook a potato by putting it into the coals of a campfire. I dug my potato out of the embers, but it wasn't completely cooked. My scoutmaster didn't accept it. My older and higher ranked friend saw that I was downcast and tried to encourage me. Finally he said, "Oh heck, that's good enough," and he signed off my requirement card. I thought that was pretty cool and went off to do other requirements.

When it was time to be reviewed for promotion in rank, my scoutmaster said, "How did that cooking requirement get signed off? I didn't sign you off!" I explained that my friend okayed it. My scoutmaster was unimpressed with this end-run around his authority. He informed me, to my acute embarrassment, that my higher-ranked friend did not have authority to sign me off. My now-vanished peace and relief were not founded on authority, but on the advice of a well-meaning pretender. His mercy wasn't mercy because it wasn't his place to hand out mercy. The only one qualified to be merciful was not inclined to let me slide through. He insisted that I fulfill the requirements. Isaiah 57:20–21 says,

> **But the wicked are like the troubled sea,**
> **When it cannot rest,**
> **Whose waters cast up mire and dirt.**
> **"There is no peace,"**
> **Says my God, "for the wicked."**

Why is there no peace for the wicked? Why can't we just forgive one another for our sins? Because we have first sinned against God by breaking His law, and only He has authority to forgive sins. God has provided forgiveness through Jesus dying on the cross. All our sins were placed on Him. His death satisfied the justice of God. A righteous penalty has been paid.

26

Therefore, there is real forgiveness for sinners. We can be accepted, forgiven, and reconciled to God through Jesus.

Those away from God might counsel one another, become sober, functional, successful, mindful, and well-adjusted. But they are not accepted by God, and He will not give them peace. Their sins are retained regardless of anything they believe to be true—whether atheism, humanism, or philosophy. A philosopher may say, "I think this is the right way to live," but his say-so doesn't make it true. Where is his authority? After all, he is just another human being.

Lack of authority means lack of power. We can list 10,000 good suggestions we ought to accomplish, but we don't have the power to carry them out. We ought to be better educated, have better health, and have better government. We should be better people, but we're not. We're helpless.

Stuck on a wrong path

The wicked stand in the path of sinners, and that's a double problem. First, the path goes away from God. Second, the wicked are firmly fixed in that path.

Any path leading away from God is wrong. It can even go in diametrically opposed directions, because anywhere away from the center of a target is still a miss. "Enter by the narrow gate; for wide is the gate and broad is the way that leads to destruction, and there are many who go in by it. Because narrow is the gate and difficult is the way which leads to life, and there are few who find it" (Matthew 7:13–14).

It should scare us to find ourselves fixed and immovable on the path away from God and life. It's hard to change a person who is convinced that he is right. Sin is hardening and

27

deceptive. "Do you see a man wise in his own eyes? There is more hope for a fool than for him" (Proverbs 26:12).

In Proverbs, a fool is not intellectually deficient, he is morally deficient. He has thrown away God's standard of right and wrong. One can be intelligent and still be a fool. But worse than being a fool is to be wise in one's own eyes. That person is proud.

With pride comes ignorance. A proud person thinks he's better than he really is. Because he knows he's superior, he won't learn anything from his inferiors. It would be damaging to his self-image. Arrogance and ignorance always walk hand in hand. Have you ever met anyone like that? Have you been that person?

If you've learned anything of value, it probably was the hard way. Instead of learning directly from a teacher or a book, you went ahead and did something you now regret. You learned, but you became humbler in the process.

If you don't learn from anything you experience, you're going to ruin your life. Wisdom really is with the humble. A proud person is headed straight for destruction. "Pride goes before destruction, and a haughty spirit before a fall" (Proverbs 16:18).

Psalm 1:1 says a wicked person sits in the seat of the scornful. He looks down on others. He criticizes and has a low opinion of nearly everything. He thinks he knows what he is doing. But he will find that the things he has trusted in will fail him. It's a double whammy. Arrogance and ignorance lead to disillusionment and cynicism.

To sum up, the wicked—those who are going away from God—are arrogant and ignorant. Anyone who thinks they know how to live better than the Author of life is arrogant and ignorant. Anyone who sets themself up as an authority in the place of God is arrogant and ignorant. Anyone who is wise in their own eyes and rejects God is arrogant and ignorant.

Blessing begins with repentance

The blessing of God begins with humbling myself and repenting of that fatal attitude: I know what I'm doing.

Remember the centurion who crucified Jesus? What would he say if you had asked him, "Sir, do you really understand what you are doing?" I bet he would say, "What does it look like I'm doing? I'm nailing this condemned scum to a piece of wood! Are you trying to tell me I don't know my job? Beat it!"

But the centurion was not arrogant; therefore, he learned something valuable. He was used to watching men die badly. But he'd never seen any crucified criminal say, "Father, forgive them; they don't know what they are doing!" This Man did not think of Himself but of others. He lived out His last moments in triumph and peace.

> **So when the centurion, who stood opposite Him, saw that He cried out like this and breathed His last, he said, "Truly this Man was the Son of God!"** (Mark 15:39)

Now ask the centurion, "Sir, do you understand what you did?"

He would have replied, "I was ignorant like a beast!"

That's the change of mind we need as well, to go from "I know what I'm doing" to "I didn't know what I was doing!" That is repentance.

In order to be blessed, we repent. We reject whatever advice ungodly people give us to find life. We turn back to God in our heart and mind and actions and go His way. A humble person learns, goes the right way, and achieves not his own glory but the glory of God.

We humble ourselves under God's mighty hand because humility receives grace from God.

If you turn away from what comes from men, from what is arrogant and ignorant and leads to death, what do you turn to?

You turn to that which has authority, humbles you, and gives you eternal life. You saturate yourself with the living Word of God by meditating on it day and night. That's the subject of the next chapter.

NOTES

1   https://historyheist.com/
    mao-political-power-grows-out-of-the-barrel-of-a-gun/

Psalm 1:2 But his delight is in the law of the LORD,
and in His law he meditates day and night.

3

Blessing through Meditating

SO FAR, YOU AGREE WITH THE PSALMIST when he writes, "Blessed is the man who walks not in the counsel of the ungodly, nor stands in the path of sinners, nor sits in the seat of the scornful" (Psalm 1:1). But it's not that easy, is it? You know the power of sin in your life. You've experienced Romans 7:18–24; you do those things you do not want to do. You know futility and wretchedness by experience. How do you quit the way of sin when it seems impossible?

The answer is Psalm 1:2, to delight in the law of the Lord and meditate in it day and night. Meditation in the law of God brings delight and prepares you to do the law of God, which results in blessing now and eternally.

Delight is paralleled with meditating

Hebrew poetry does not generally rhyme the sounds of words;

instead, it compares and contrasts ideas. One line states an idea, and the next line may repeat the idea in different words or contrast it with a different idea. This is called parallelism.

These two lines in Psalm 1:2 are parallel—they describe the same thought with different words. Notice "delight" is paralleled with "meditate." Verbs show action.

Here are two things you can and should do with the law of the Lord: delight in it and meditate in it.

The last step of digestion

Meditating is for the mind what digestion is for the body—it's how you receive inwardly what you need to live.

To digest, you chew your food, enjoy the taste, and then swallow it. Your stomach adds enzymes and acids to further break down the food into its constituent elements: amino acids, fats, glucose (the simplest sugar), minerals, and vitamins. Then in the intestines, the elements are absorbed into the body and distributed as needed. In particular, glucose circulates through the body in the blood system to be absorbed into the cells. Finally, the pancreas secretes insulin, a hormone that sends a chemical message to the body's cells, telling them to open up and take in glucose.

Suppose your body didn't get that chemical message? You would die. In type-1 diabetes, the body has lost the cells that produce insulin. A type-1 diabetic eats and digests properly, but they must manually calculate and inject the correct amount of insulin to cause the cells to absorb glucose. Without insulin, the accumulated glucose becomes too much for the system and is flushed from the body by the kidneys. Food goes through the person, not into the person.

If diabetes is not treated, the cells will run out of sugar and begin burning stored fat, releasing toxic ketones into the blood. Before a diabetic starves to death, these toxins kill him. Who would imagine that missing the last step of digestion could be fatal?

In a similar way, it's possible for you to read the Bible and study it but not receive any benefit, because you don't take the last step of inwardly receiving it. It's as though you haven't read at all. But when you meditate on the Scriptures, you complete that last step to receive those words into the deepest part of your heart. Just as food becomes a part of you when you eat it, God's Word becomes a part of your heart when you meditate on it. The will of God no longer comes from outside of you, but it lives in you. You do the will of God from the heart. We'll expand on this in the next chapter.

The law of the Lord is delightful?

Someone might say, "I thought the law was all a bunch of do's and don'ts and who begat who. Where's the delight there?" That echoes the counsel of the ungodly. After all, how could obeying God's law be fun?

But this is something beyond mere fun or entertainment. We're talking about blessing which leads to eternal life. Remember, anything less than eternal life is a stay of execution.

The psalmist testified in Psalm 119:97–104:

> [97] **Oh, how I love Your law!**
> **It is my meditation all the day.**
> [98] **You, through Your commandments, make me wiser**

than my enemies;
For they are ever with me.
[99] I have more understanding than all my teachers,
For Your testimonies are my meditation.
[100] I understand more than the ancients,
Because I keep Your precepts.
[101] I have restrained my feet from every evil way,
That I may keep Your word.
[102] I have not departed from Your judgments,
For You Yourself have taught me.
[103] How sweet are Your words to my taste,
Sweeter than honey to my mouth!
[104] Through Your precepts I get understanding;
Therefore I hate every false way.

Never gets old

Notice how the psalmist doesn't get tired of the Word of God?
You can get tired of music, movies, games, and books. *Lord of
the Rings* can bore you. You can't listen to *Kind of Blue* one
more time. But God's Word delights continually. When you
meditate on it, you are putting something eternal into your
innermost being. Eternity never gets old.

You become more

In verses 98–100, the psalmist says he understands more than
his enemies, his teachers, and even the aged ancients with all
their experience. The law of the Lord gives the wisdom, insight,
and understanding of God Himself, who transcends all. A man
can be outnumbered by his enemies but overcome them

through the insight that comes from the law of the Lord. A man will rise higher than his teachers when he learns from God Himself. And though we respect the ancients, it is possible that they missed a point. The Holy Spirit can teach a man something today that He did not show to Charles Spurgeon.

Taught to hold fast to the right way

In verses 101–102, the psalmist realizes that he has to avoid evil if he goes God's way. He chooses and holds to that way because God Himself impresses it on his heart through His Word. Imagine God taking time to teach you on a regular basis. He causes you to understand simply and memorably. His insights stay with you and shape your life. You will not quickly leave His way.

Sweetness and satisfaction

The Word of God is sweeter than honey, says the psalmist in Psalm 119:103. We may wonder, *How could that be?* Because all that is in the Law can be expressed in two commandments: "You shall love the LORD your God with all your heart, with all your soul, and with all your mind" and "You shall love your neighbor as yourself" (Matthew 22:37, 39). A life lived in the love of God is sweet and satisfying. No one was ever satisfied with a life of sin and rebellion against God.

Jesus said, "It is more blessed to give than to receive" (Acts 20:35). This truth is woven into the fabric of the universe. If you want to be blessed, then give to someone. Make someone else's life better. Live in love.

The prerequisite is that you are connected to a source of love that doesn't run dry. Otherwise, you will be squeezed out like an old toothpaste tube, and that's no fun. When you meditate, you are connected to the fountain of living water. There's more about that in Psalm 1, which we will look at in our next chapter.

If you don't meditate, you won't do

The biblical order of obedience is this: meditate on the Word of God, receive it inwardly, and then do it from the heart. If you are not doing the will of God, don't beat yourself up. You're behind on your think time. Check to see if you are consistently meditating on the will of God that you are failing to do. Meditating prepares your heart for doing. You do what you meditate on.

This also works the other way. It's why there are books, music, videos, and movies that present rebellious, sinful ideas. Murder, adultery, jealousy, revenge, hatred, self-centeredness, lust—our entertainment features them all. Entertain, by the way, means to maintain, keep, or hold in the mind. The devil wants to keep sinful ideas in your mind so you will do them. If you meditate on sinful things, don't be surprised if you eventually do them.

You can choose what you think about. You are not a victim; you are a volunteer. What are you volunteering for? What do you set your mind on? Philippians 3:18–19 says,

> **For many walk, of whom I have told you often, and now tell you even weeping, that they are the enemies of the cross of Christ: whose end is destruction, whose god is their belly, and whose glory is in their shame—who set their mind on earthly things.**

Paul knew people who were busy working against their own salvation. It grieved him that they were stubborn and unwilling to consider their ways and change their thoughts.

Challenge yourself

Here's a challenge: if you believe in Jesus, and you want to experience His goodness, then delight in His Word for the next thirty days.

It might be a good time for a media blackout to get your taste buds recalibrated for the Word of God.

When the Israelites left Egypt, they complained about the manna God gave them to eat (Numbers 11:4–9). Manna tasted like wafers made with oil. It was good, but evidently it didn't register on Israel's taste buds. They were used to more zip, bang, and pow in their food, with garlic, leeks, and fish. That's like eating all your food with siracha and tabasco sauce. Israel was discontent because they couldn't taste God's bread from heaven.

Is the Bible tasteless to you? Maybe it's because you're conditioned to all the zip, bang, and pow in your media. Advertisers, writers, marketers, and video producers aim at stimulating your body's dopamine production. They want you to become addicted to a media-saturated lifestyle.

In a world of things that scream for your attention, the Bible is not one of them. God will not lunge at you or compete with marketers for your attention. Did you notice that when He spoke to Elijah, He wasn't in the raging wind or the earthquake or the blazing fire? Instead, He spoke in a still, small voice (1 Kings 19:11–12). To those who are accustomed to incessant media, God's whisper is silent and flat.

When people tell me they want to hear from God, I often suggest, "Get desperate. Cut out all the stuff you allow into your life that has nothing to do with Jesus. The blogs, news sources, chat groups, forums, magazines, music, and videos may not be bad in themselves, but what do they have in common with Jesus?" For this particular time of seeking the Lord, I even suggest cutting out Christian media. The good can be the enemy of the best. The best is you receiving from God Himself. Nothing else compares when He speaks.

For the sake of the challenge, be brutal. Make it just you and the Bible.

Read through books of the Bible, a number of chapters every day. Experiment to find your daily capacity, an amount you can read that isn't too much for you or too little. If a verse starts talking to you, take time to listen and consider. In a notebook, verbalize your observations, your questions, and other Bible verses as they occur to you. Ask God to fill you with the Holy Spirit and give you insight. Pray about the things you learn.

You'll probably experience some nasty cold turkey withdrawal from the media you cut out. Don't feel bad about it. After all, you're still in the body. At the same time, God will satisfy you more and more. You'll get hungry for Him to speak to your heart. You'll find yourself delighting in the law of the Lord.

Do you think it will take thirty days for God to start speaking to you? I doubt it. I think you'll have a fabulous time of communion with Him.

What you do after the fast is totally up to you. But consider the long run. What do you think would happen if your top priority was to meditate in the Bible for the rest of your life? The answer is in the next chapter: seriously transcendent, wonderful, glorious things worth more than everything in this life.

Psalm 1:3 He shall be like a tree planted by the rivers of water, that brings forth its fruit in its season, whose leaf also shall not wither; and whatever he does shall prosper.

4

What's So Cool about Being a Tree?

I AM NOT a "word of faith" guy. I have lived long enough to know that God doesn't promise extreme material wealth and health. But what He does promise is true prosperity, the life that comes through meditating in His Scriptures. God begins Psalm 1 with a promise of blessing. Now in verse 3, He defines that blessing.

Be a tree

I don't think anyone in his right mind ever wanted to be a tree. Rock star, yes. Science wiz, yes. Nintendo geek, yes.

Tree, no.

So what's so cool about being a tree?

Radical transformation.

> The voice said, "Cry out!"
> And he said, "What shall I cry?"
> "All flesh is grass,
> And all its loveliness is like the flower of the field.
> The grass withers, the flower fades,
> Because the breath of the LORD blows upon it;
> Surely the people are grass.
> The grass withers, the flower fades,
> But the word of our God stands forever." (Isaiah 40:6–8)

All flesh is like grass—temporary, here today, gone tomorrow. Trees are different.

> "For there is hope for a tree,
> If it is cut down, that it will sprout again,
> And that its tender shoots will not cease.
> Though its root may grow old in the earth,
> And its stump may die in the ground,
> Yet at the scent of water it will bud
> And bring forth branches like a plant.
> But man dies and is laid away;
> Indeed he breathes his last
> And where is he?
> As water disappears from the sea,
> And a river becomes parched and dries up,
> So man lies down and does not rise.
> Till the heavens are no more,
> They will not awake
> Nor be roused from their sleep." (Job 14:7–12)

Chop down a tree and it will live again. Trees can come back from the dead. Grass and men don't do that. Do you see your need? Every one of us needs to be radically transformed from being grass to a tree.

Flesh can't radically transform itself

Nothing you do can change you from being grass to a tree. It's humanly impossible to change your essential nature.

Experts say no, you can finally have peace with yourself—be something else. Change into whatever you want to be happy. It's more than reseeding hair, looking taller, or losing weight. You can change gender. Men, you can be women and have babies. You can have sexual relations with anyone or anything or nothing. You can do anything you want to be happy. There are no boundaries.

Devotees of this agenda trust the experts and leap by faith into new regions, expecting a soft landing. Instead, they smash themselves against God's immutable boundaries. Saying that there are no boundaries doesn't make them go away.

These attempts are sincere but hopelessly superficial. A person might order radical surgical additions or deletions to themselves, but that doesn't change what is written in each of their billion cells. Cutting and stitching only alter the appearance, not the essence. You don't take a blade of grass, color its stem brown, cut a leaf shape out of green paper, tape it to the blade, and say, "Voilá! You're a tree!" Wearing a tree t-shirt isn't enough. Either you're a tree or you're not.

> **I have seen the wicked in great power,**
> **And spreading himself like a native green tree.**

Yet he passed away, and behold, he was no more;
Indeed I sought him, but he could not be found.
(Psalm 37:35–36)

The wicked make themselves out to be trees. They might look like trees. Some dictators live and live and live. But in the end, they die like any other person. They are grass after all.

Here's a radical solution

Why not rewrite the DNA in all your billion cells so that what is wrong is made right? If you change the DNA, you change the essential person, right?

If you could, yeah, but this is impossible.

Can the Ethiopian change his skin or the leopard its spots? Then may you also do good who are accustomed to do evil. (Jeremiah 13:23)

You can't counsel an Ethiopian or a leopard to get a bucket of paint and a 6-inch brush. Skin-deep solutions don't work. Both the skin color of an Ethiopian and the spots of a leopard are determined by the DNA in every one of their cells.

The Bible testifies that our essential nature rebels against God. We are sinners from birth. We are born grass. So how in the world can we change our essential nature and become trees?

God does the impossible

God can actually rewrite our spiritual DNA so we will really be trees and not deceive ourselves. He begins with new life through new birth. God is not interested in refurbishing a corrupted, temporary life. He gives eternal life in Christ.

> For God so loved the world that He gave His only begotten Son, that whoever believes in Him should not perish but have everlasting life. For God did not send His Son into the world to condemn the world, but that the world through Him might be saved. (John 3:16–17)

He calls us to turn around and receive the new birth by receiving Jesus.

> But as many as received Him, to them He gave the right to become children of God, to those who believe in His name: who were born, not of blood, nor of the will of the flesh, nor of the will of man, but of God (John 1:12–13).

Receiving Jesus begins our new life. We become a new creation of God.

> Therefore, if anyone is in Christ, he is a new creation; old things have passed away; behold, all things have become new. (2 Corinthians 5:17).

So far, we have passed through a crisis, a turning point. We were dead in our sins, separated from God. We stopped going away from Him, we turned around and started going the opposite way. We are born again spiritually.

God begins a process of renewing our minds to think like Christ. It is not immediate, like being born again. It would be less hassle and a lot faster if it were. But relationships require time to develop intellectually, emotionally, and practically. We have come into a new relationship of life with the Father through Jesus. His next step is to make us new in our minds.

I beseech you therefore, brethren, by the mercies of God, that you present your bodies a living sacrifice, holy, acceptable to God, which is your reasonable service. And do not be conformed to this world, but be transformed by the renewing of your mind, that you may prove what is that good and acceptable and perfect will of God. (Romans 12:1–2)

You will grow in understanding God's mercies. You will grow in spiritual and rational worship. You will shake off being conformed to the way this dark and fallen world thinks. All this happens as your mind is renewed.

God's Word shows you how to think and live. Your life is defined and guided by what He says. When you receive the thoughts of God, He fulfills His will.

**Seek the LORD while He may be found,
Call upon Him while He is near.
Let the wicked forsake his way,
And the unrighteous man his thoughts;
Let him return to the LORD,
And He will have mercy on him;
And to our God,
For He will abundantly pardon.
"For My thoughts are not your thoughts,**

46

Nor are your ways My ways," says the LORD.
For as the heavens are higher than the earth,
So are My ways higher than your ways,
And My thoughts than your thoughts.
For as the rain comes down, and the snow from heaven,
And do not return there,
But water the earth,
And make it bring forth and bud,
That it may give seed to the sower
And bread to the eater,
So shall My word be that goes forth from My mouth;
It shall not return to Me void,
But it shall accomplish what I please,
And it shall prosper in the thing for which I sent it."
(Isaiah 55:6–11)

"God said, 'Let there be light'; and there was light'" (Genesis
1:3). That same powerful Word transforms the wicked into the
righteous. He succeeds because His Word always accomplishes
what He sends it to do.

This is different from listening to motivational recordings
that lead you to say, "I am a champion. I am successful. Day
by day, in every way, I am getting better and better." Thinking
a thing does not make it so. What you think must first be true.

We will be transformed from temporary grass to permanent
trees as we meditate in the truth day and night.

Trees don't plant themselves

I can visualize an old-growth forest, thickly wooded, growing
randomly. But if I see trees planted in rows, each carefully

trimmed and cultivated, I know that behind the beauty, someone is working.

The verb used in Psalm 1 for "planted" is a passive participle. This means I don't do the action, the action is done to me. So if I'm not doing the planting, who is?

> **To console those who mourn in Zion,**
> **To give them beauty for ashes,**
> **The oil of joy for mourning,**
> **The garment of praise for the spirit of heaviness;**
> **That they may be called trees of righteousness,**
> **The planting of the Lord, that He may be glorified."**
> (Isaiah 61:3)

The answer is God—the gardener, vinedresser, and cultivator of His people. He created them, He redeems them, He disciplines them, He shapes and molds their character. God's people are His workmanship, His inheritance, His possession. When you think about what God does, you have to get your head around this: God's work comes before your work. Whatever you do is based upon what He has already done and is still doing. You meditate, that's for sure. But God is the One who plants and cultivates His tree, which you are.

Superabundant provision

A tree planted next to rivers of water has a superabundant supply. One river would be plenty for a tree. In fact, a forest of trees could drink from the river, and you would never know that the river felt the drain. Rivers are God's way of saying there's more where that came from.

But here it says, "planted by rivers," plural. God has more to give than you can handle. He won't run dry and neither will you. Notice also that water is symbolic of the Holy Spirit.

On the last day, that great day of the feast, Jesus stood and cried out, saying, "If anyone thirsts, let him come to Me and drink. He who believes in Me, as the Scripture has said, out of his heart will flow rivers of living water." But this He spoke concerning the Spirit, whom those believing in Him would receive; for the Holy Spirit was not yet given, because Jesus was not yet glorified. (John 7:37–39)

Jesus connects the Holy Spirit with His Word.

It is the Spirit who gives life; the flesh profits nothing. The words that I speak to you are spirit, and they are life. (John 6:63)

For the word of God is living and powerful, and sharper than any two-edged sword, piercing even to the division of soul and spirit, and of joints and marrow, and is a discerner of the thoughts and intents of the heart. (Hebrews 4:12)

Notice the similarity of these verses:

And do not be drunk with wine, in which is dissipation; but be filled with the Spirit, speaking to one another in psalms and hymns and spiritual songs, singing and

making melody in your heart to the Lord.
(Ephesians 5:18–19)

Let the word of Christ dwell in you richly in all wisdom, teaching and admonishing one another in psalms and hymns and spiritual songs, singing with grace in your hearts to the Lord. (Colossians 3:16)

It is the Spirit who gives life; the flesh profits nothing. The words that I speak to you are spirit, and they are life. (John 6:63)

When you fill yourself with the Word, you will also be filling yourself with the Spirit. Some people make a false division between the Spirit and the Word, as though focusing on the Word of God was some dry, dusty academic exercise, like the letter of the Old Testament law, "which kills." But the verse goes on to say that "the Spirit gives life" (2 Corinthians 3:6).

I was patronized once by a Pentecostal who told me, "You have your little Bible studies, but WE have the freedom of the Spirit!" Remember that the Holy Spirit spoke to men to write the Word of God (2 Peter 1:21). It's unspiritual to ignore what God has said. God has joined His Spirit and His Word together; let no man separate them. So the most spiritual thing you can do is sow the Word of God into your mind and heart.

Now hope does not disappoint, because the love of God has been poured out in our hearts by the Holy Spirit who was given to us. (Romans 5:5)

Scripture also connects the Holy Spirit with God's love. Love is not a thing in itself. God is love (1 John 4:8). Love is a person. The Spirit communicates His everlasting love to us.

Love is the best part of life. Moses found he could flourish on a 38-year death march to kill two million complainers, eating only manna, as long as God satisfied him with eternal love.

O satisfy us in the morning with Your lovingkindness,
That we may sing for joy and be glad all our days.
(Psalm 90:14 NASB1995)

Put everything good in life on one side and put God's love on the other. What do you choose, David? David immediately says, "Lovingkindness." It's better than everything in life.

Because Your lovingkindness is better than life,
My lips shall praise You. (Psalm 63:3)

But David, you suffer setbacks, things don't work out, and you make mistakes! How will you ever pick yourself up off the floor?

If I should say, "My foot has slipped,"
Your lovingkindness, O LORD, will hold me up.
(Psalm 94:18 NASB1995)

Wow. Would you like to live with that kind of love? You will when you meditate.

Guaranteed fruitfulness in season

God is going to make you into a fruit tree. Fruit is for others, not for the tree. You never saw an apple tree enjoy its own fruit. Trees are others-oriented. They feed people. God will teach you and show you things that will nourish your soul. What you receive you can pass on to others.

The fruit that this tree bears is love. Love is about being focused on others, not yourself. As you receive God's love, it will overflow into loving others, giving yourself to others, and benefitting others.

A tree bears fruit in its season. God made trees to be consistent. You will become consistent as you partake of God.

I can't tell you how many times I have meditated in my little morning time, and later that day God allowed me to feed someone with what I learned. It might have been a big-name person or a no-name missionary or a cashier in a clothing store who isn't a Christian.

Food is fabulous when it's fresh. Truth nourishes the same whether the hearer is a believer or not, simply because it's true. It makes hearts leap for joy, just like when Jesus taught the disciples on the road to Emmaus (Luke 24:13-14).

In John 15, Jesus spoke of His Father as the vinedresser. Your Father is a farmer who works the earth and cultivates fruit. He prunes you, a branch in Jesus, to make you fruitful. A vinedresser knows where to cut a branch so there will be young canes of the right age to bear fruit. He cuts away unproductive shoots. He also cuts away dead branches. The sharp blade the Father uses is His Word. As you continually expose yourself to the Word, His sharp blade keeps you fruitful.

Nourishment from above

Trees are solar-powered miracles. They photosynthesize, using radiant energy to create glucose and starch. Trees live on light from the heavens. So you, too, live on the light and the life that comes from meditating on the Scriptures.

In Him was life, and the life was the light of men. (John 1:4)

The entrance of Your words gives light;
It gives understanding to the simple. (Psalm 119:130)

The kind of tree spoken of in Psalm 1 is an evergreen tree, which keeps its leaves all year round. Fruit grows in season, but evergreens nourish themselves every day of the year. Like a tree, you're not dependent on your environment or circumstances. The light of God is always there to give you life. You live in God's light.

But you are a chosen generation, a royal priesthood, a holy nation, His own special people, that you may proclaim the praises of Him who called you out of darkness into His marvelous light (1 Peter 2:9).

Believers are most often compared to evergreens, with one notable exception in Isaiah 44:4. There, the one who has received the Spirit is like a willow by the watercourses. It's not a miracle for a willow to grow by a river. But the context shows that God is pouring out His Spirit on dry ground in the wilderness (that's us). The miracle is that a tree without an apparent source of water flourishes in the desert, leaving onlookers mystified: "Where is the river? How does it do that?" They look downward where rivers usually are, but the source of this river of life is from above.

The true promise of success

When the psalmist says in Psalm 1:3, "And whatever he does shall prosper," we move past the tree metaphor to a point-blank promise of success: All that you do will prosper. This sounds too good to be true, a "word of faith" twisting of the Word of God. However, this is a most sober promise.

You will prosper because when you meditate on the Word of God, you will do the Word of God from your heart. God defines success as doing His will.

Meditation prepares you for doing

We see this in Joshua 1:6–8:

> **Be strong and of good courage, for to this people you shall divide as an inheritance the land which I swore to their fathers to give them. Only be strong and very courageous, that you may observe to do according to all the law which Moses My servant commanded you; do not turn from it to the right hand or to the left, that you may prosper wherever you go. This Book of the Law shall not depart from your mouth, but you shall meditate in it day and night, that you may observe to do according to all that is written in it. For then you will make your way prosperous, and then you will have good success.**

Notice first what God told Joshua to do: bring the people of Israel into the Promised Land to possess it. That was a big job. Moses couldn't do that!

Then God told Joshua the way to do it: follow the law of Moses. The people were to possess the land by doing what God says.

And then God told Joshua how to obey the law of Moses: always meditate on it. As he received God's law in his inner man, God fulfilled His word and gave Joshua success.

What you think, you will do

Meditating prepares you for doing. Thinking leads to action. You do what you think about. God intends that you think deeply on His will before you do it. The proper order is to meditate, then do.

Doing without meditating is not the biblical order. If you find that your doing is not according to the Word of God, it's probably because you're behind on your "think" time, and you're thinking of something other than God's Word.

If you think enough about sin, you will commit sin. The postal worker who bought a 12-gauge shotgun, killed his co-workers, and then killed himself had mulled it over for years before he finally did it. The thinkable became doable.

Imagine a wedding ceremony where the pastor asks the new couple when they're getting their divorce. "What?" they protest. "That's inconceivable! We just got married! We're in love! We're not going to split up!"

But sometime down the road they stop thinking of marriage and start thinking of divorce. The unthinkable becomes thinkable, and the thinkable becomes doable.

I heard the story of a pastor who saw a woman come into his congregation and thought, *Boy, would I like to sleep with her!* He thought about it for five years. Then he did it.

The battles of your life take place first in your heart. That's where you must defend yourself.

> **Keep your heart with all diligence,**
> **For out of it spring the issues of life.** (Proverbs 4:23)

The best defence is a good offense. Nourish and satisfy your heart by meditating on the Word of God. The Holy Spirit will write that Word on your heart and make it part of you, deep inside. Then you will do the will of God from your heart.

Column A and Column B are really the same thing

Accomplishing God's will defines success for all eternity. But we have to understand what the will of God is and what it isn't. Stick with me as I unbox this.

The writer to the Hebrews lists heroes of faith and then adds this:

> **And what more shall I say? For the time would fail me to tell of Gideon and Barak and Samson and Jephthah, also of David and Samuel and the prophets: who through faith subdued kingdoms, worked righteousness, obtained promises, stopped the mouths of lions, quenched the violence of fire, escaped the edge of the sword, out of weakness were made strong, became valiant in battle, turned to flight the armies of the aliens. Women received**

their dead raised to life again. Others were tortured, not accepting deliverance, that they might obtain a better resurrection. Still others had trial of mockings and scourgings, yes, and of chains and imprisonment. They were stoned, they were sawn in two, were tempted, were slain with the sword. They wandered about in sheepskins and goatskins, being destitute, afflicted, tormented— of whom the world was not worthy. They wandered in deserts and mountains, in dens and caves of the earth. (Hebrews 11:32–38)

These unnamed people can be divided into Column A and Column B.

Column A has the miracles we like to see: answered prayer, protection in danger, battles won, miracles of resurrection.

Column B has things hard to understand: torture, death, mocking, scourging, imprisonment, stoning, execution, not-very-nice clothing, poverty.

Everyone I know wants to be in Column A. Who wouldn't?

Most of us find ourselves in Column B. What's the deal?

Both columns have a common denominator, which is doing the will of God. God's will for some people is to be miraculous, victorious, and delivered. God's will for others is that they suffer and die. Health and wealth teachers would say that Column A is the norm, and you don't have enough faith if you're in Column B. That's not true. Both columns are equally valid.

We count the major prophets as successful Column A types. But tradition says that the one sawed in two was Isaiah. And God told Isaiah that no one would believe him (Isaiah 6:8–11). When God called Jeremiah, He made it clear that the people would resist him and fight against him (Jeremiah 1:8, 18–19). He was mocked, beaten, put in stocks, imprisoned, and thrown in an empty cistern to die. The Lord made sure Ezekiel knew that though people gathered and listened to him, they weren't taking the word to heart. They listened to Ezekiel as if he were a musician playing for their entertainment (Ezekiel 33:30–33). Stephen emphasizes what we would consider unsuccessful ministry of the prophets in Acts 7:51–53: "You stiff-necked and uncircumcised in heart and ears! You always resist the Holy Spirit; as your fathers did, so do you. Which of the prophets did your fathers not persecute? And they killed those who foretold the coming of the Just One, of whom you now have become the betrayers and murderers, who have received the law by the direction of angels and have not kept it."

John the Baptist experienced Column A ministry. He began as an unknown, crying out in the wilderness. He didn't go to people; people came out to him. He dealt with multitudes. Decades after John's death his disciples were found as far away as Ephesus in Asia Minor (Acts 19:1-3). Yet John also experienced Column B. John peaked at age 30 after pointing to Jesus as the Lamb of God. Disciples began leaving him and following Jesus. John's disciples watched their ministry diminish in favor of the newcomer.

John answered and said, "A man can receive nothing unless it has been given to him from heaven." (John 3:27)

John descended to being arrested, left in prison, and executed. We look at John's life and wonder, What was that all about? No wife, no kids, no legacy. Dead at age 30. That's it?

What do you think he felt like just after being beheaded? Imagine yourself standing in heaven five minutes later, trying to help John process this painful event.

"Wow, John, big bummer, man. Getting beheaded and everything. Yeesh, not so good, huh? Too bad, man. Wow. I really feel for you."

I think John would have looked at you and yelled, "Are you CRAZY? I just saw GOD! He said, 'WELL DONE, GOOD AND FAITHFUL SERVANT!' I fulfilled the will of God! If I had to die a thousand times, I'd do it all again!"

Here's the clincher: the Author and Finisher of our faith is both Column A and Column B. Jesus preached to thousands, performed miracles, and healed multitudes. He was also arrested, scourged, and crucified. His death was expressly the will of God, as Isaiah says:

> **Yet it pleased the LORD to bruise Him;**
> **He has put Him to grief.**
> **When You make His soul an offering for sin,**
> **He shall see His seed, He shall prolong His days,**
> **And the pleasure of the LORD shall prosper in His hand.**
> (Isaiah 53:10)

So what?

I once saw this post on social media: "Work-obsessed billionaire dying of cancer wants to say, 'Friends, relationships, and cherishing the moment is what life is all about.'" It sounds straight out of the movie "It's A Wonderful Life," and yet it's completely wrong. Where is doing the will of God in all that? Eternal life is yielding yourself to Jesus Christ and doing His will, whatever He has for you. Jesus told the church of Smyrna, "Be faithful until death" (Revelation 2:10). Then you will receive the eternal inheritance, "incorruptible and undefiled...reserved in heaven for you" (1 Peter 1:4). You will receive that "living hope" (1 Peter 1:3), the glory of Jesus Himself. That's what life is about.

God's specific will looks different for each one of us. That's why we can't compare ourselves to see how we're doing. It's not about who the winners and losers are. It's about doing what God wants you to do. If you look successful to others, they might congratulate you because you are in Column A. And if you look like a failure, people may write you off because—well, dear— you *are* in Column B. Sorry you're such a loser.

How God rates you is everything.

Who cares what anyone else thinks?

Pursue the will of God. Meditate on His Word. Do what He says. But what happens if you don't meditate?

That's the subject of our next chapter.

Psalm 1:4-5 The ungodly are not so, but are like the chaff which the wind drives away. Therefore the ungodly shall not stand in the judgment, nor sinners in the congregation of the righteous.

5

It Is Horrible to Be Chaff

MAYBE YOU'RE THINKING of meditating. You're asking yourself, "Do I want to commit to this or not? What happens if I do it? What happens if I don't?"

If you meditate, you experience the life of God. The blessings go off the chart.

What happens if you don't meditate in the Bible? The short answer is you have no life of God in you. You are like chaff.

So what? What does that look like?

The wicked are not so

You are not like the righteous, says the psalmist in verse 4. Without a vital connection to the life of God, you are not properly alive. You exist but not as God made you to be.

In the beginning God took the dust of the earth, made a

man, breathed the breath of life into that man, and the man became a living being (Genesis 2:7). That breath of God is His Spirit. The Hebrew language uses one word to express both breath and spirit, as does the Greek. We were created by God to be indwelt by His Holy Spirit. That's what it was to be normal in the Garden of Eden.

When man sinned against God, he became abnormal. God said, "But of the tree of the knowledge of good and evil you shall not eat, for in the day that you eat of it you shall surely die" (Genesis 2:17). Adam and Eve didn't keel over dead physically, but they died spiritually. Their spiritual connection with God was broken. The lamp of God in them, His Spirit, went out. They were plunged into darkness. They instinctively knew they were naked and cut off from God. For them, Eden became like Jurassic Park. When they heard God walking in the garden in the cool of the day, they reacted as if He were Tyrannosaurus rex and dived into the bushes.

When God confronts us in our sinful condition, our natural instinct is to run. We think, *Don't let Him get us! Avoid all mention of Him.* We're afraid He'll take from us, shame us, or embarrass us. We actively maintain that disconnect from Him.

But are like the chaff which the wind drives away

Chaff is the outside husk of a grain, such as wheat. When wheat is harvested, chaff must be removed by threshing.

In the psalmist's time, harvested grain was spread on a threshing floor, which was a raised area, like the top of a hill. Then a thresher (a roller studded with spikes) was hitched to a bull or a donkey, which was chained to a central post. The animal walked around the post while dragging the thresher behind it, breaking up the outer husk from the grain inside. To separate the grain from the outer husk, the farmer tossed the grain into the air with his pitchfork.

Even a light breeze would blow the chaff downwind, away from the grain, as the grain dropped back down to the threshing floor. Eventually the chaff would blow away and only the grain remained.

To sum up, chaff is what used to be alive and part of the plant, but after harvesting, it is dead.

Chaff has no nutritional value. Thus, it doesn't give life. It's temporary and has no use after the grain is harvested. It has no purpose and must be separated from the grain or the grain cannot be used. It has no weight. It is practically nothing. It's disintegrated, like dust.

It is horrible to be chaff

People disconnected from the Word of God are like chaff.

They live temporarily. Even if they live eighty or ninety years, that is nothing compared to eternity.

They have no permanent, eternal purpose. Nothing a temporary person does will last forever. What was once valuable becomes worthless. Everything is ultimately futile.

The disconnected can't give life; they only take life. Love gives life. Love lays down one's rights and privileges for the one loved, either quickly as Jesus did for us or slowly over a span of years.

You can kill fast or slow. We know about fast life-taking—bullets, knives, jumps from building tops. Slow life-taking forces other people around you to lay down their lives for you. Demand this right, deny that privilege, oppress, condemn, treat spitefully. It takes a long time to kill someone that way, but it's just as effective as a bullet.

I once explained this idea while teaching at a church, and afterward a woman told me, "That's what my grandmother did to my grandfather. She nagged, demanded, and extracted service from him. He made up his mind to divorce her once, but in the end he stayed because he didn't want her to kill someone else." The woman said her grandmother killed her grandfather just as surely as a quick murder.

The disconnected are inconsequential. That's a big word, meaning they have no impact. They're trivial.

Steve Jobs changed the way we use computers, music, phones, retail business, and watches. He built the most profitable company in the history of the world. He made a lot of money, provided employment, kept people alive, and spawned new industries and applications for computing and personal empowerment.

Did he live forever? Will his company exist forever? Will those who use his products live forever? Will the things they accomplish last forever? What's that all about in light of eternity? In the eternal scheme of things, Steve Jobs is a lightweight. Hard to imagine, yet true.

The disconnected are practically nothing, and their end is to be burned forever.

The ungodly will not stand

The disconnected won't stand in the judgment to come (Psalm 1:5). On the scales of God, they're lighter than air. They've rejected their only salvation, Jesus Christ, the Son of God. They're guilty of loving the darkness rather than the light because their deeds are evil (John 3:19). Their end is to burn. Chaff does that well. That's why we warn everyone to "flee from the wrath to come" (Matthew 3:7). Not because we think we're better, but because we, too, are fleeing that wrath. Thank God there is salvation for the guilty, that Jesus came to save sinners.

But sinners won't stand in the congregation of the righteous now, in the present. There should be a huge difference between someone who is saved and someone who is not saved.

Saved means connected to the life of God through Jesus Christ, by the indwelling of the Holy Spirit. This connection is maintained by meditating on the Word of God. A saved person manifests the character of Christ by thinking like Him and doing like Him. He said,

A new commandment I give to you, that you love one another; as I have loved you, that you also love one another. By this all will know that you are My disciples, if you have love for one another. (John 13:34–35)

By this My Father is glorified, that you bear much fruit; so you will be My disciples. (John 15:8)

But the fruit of the Spirit is love, joy, peace, longsuffering, kindness, goodness, faithfulness, gentleness, self-control. Against such there is no law. (Galatians 5:22–23)

Greater love has no one than this, than to lay down one's life for his friends. (John 15:13)

Not saved means not indwelt by the Holy Spirit, not connected to the life of God, and not laying your life down for your friends. If you aren't giving life through loving others, then you can't help taking life from those around you. That is your essential nature. You are dead chaff.

There's a huge difference between giving life and taking life. Church should be a place so full of love that anyone who doesn't love will stick out like a sore thumb. Jesus should be the focus. Our lives should revolve around Him, not ourselves.

Many years ago I saw chaff come into the church in Germany where I served. We had a baptism there, with ten people ready to take the plunge in a freezing pond. Obeying Jesus' command that day required fortitude. We were having such a great time that one fellow suddenly decided to get baptized too. He didn't have a swimsuit or a towel, but he took off his shoes and socks and jumped in. We baptized him and marvelled at the way the Lord was moving.

Over time, as we talked to people in the church, we found that they smelled a rat. The fellow was borrowing money from the men and not paying them back. He was trying to make out with the young women. His life didn't show forth the love of Jesus.

It was obvious he'd gotten baptized to join a crowd of nice people and use them to his advantage. He wasn't born again, and it wasn't a true baptism. He'd just gotten freezing wet.

Christianity is not about becoming a nice guy. Christianity is Jesus Christ living in those who have received Him. It's about loving people, giving life to them, and testifying to the truth.

Check yourself out

Are you connected to Jesus or are you one of the disconnected? Are you a branch in the vine or are you chaff? Are you someone who gives life or takes life? It's easy to look at others and evaluate them. But for this we need to look at ourselves and see how we are doing.

Do you think like Jesus? If you don't think like Him, you won't act like Him. God sees your thoughts, and that's where it starts. He weighs the motives of your heart. You appreciate everyone who likes you on social media, but ultimately their opinions don't count. You will stand before God, not people. A fearless moral inventory should reveal that you think nothing like Jesus. You think like disconnected chaff.

Let's change this. If you see how little you resemble Him, you're on the right track. Jesus said,

> **"Blessed are the poor in spirit, for theirs is the kingdom of heaven."** (Matthew 5:3)

Here's what to do: Be born again. Get the life of Jesus in you. Then build a connection to God through meditating in His Word. As you meditate, you will change the way you think. You will change the way you act.

> **Seek the LORD while He may be found,**
> **Call upon Him while He is near.**
> **Let the wicked forsake his way,**
> **And the unrighteous man his thoughts;**
> **Let him return to the LORD,**

And He will have mercy on him;
And to our God,
For He will abundantly pardon.
"For My thoughts are not your thoughts,
Nor are your ways My ways," says the LORD.
"For as the heavens are higher than the earth,
So are My ways higher than your ways,
And My thoughts than your thoughts.
For as the rain comes down, and the snow from heaven,
And do not return there,
But water the earth,
And make it bring forth and bud,
That it may give seed to the sower
And bread to the eater,
So shall My word be that goes forth from My mouth;
It shall not return to Me void,
But it shall accomplish what I please,
And it shall prosper in the thing for which I sent it."
(Isaiah 55:6–11)

Exchange your thoughts and ways for God's thoughts and ways. You will live His higher and better life. It begins when you fill yourself with His Word and let it do its work in you. You have God's guarantee that His Word always accomplishes what He sends it to do (Isaiah 55:11).

The time to do this is now. The end of the world is approaching. It says so in Psalm 1:6.

That's the subject of our next chapter.

Psalm 1:6 For the LORD knows the way of the righteous, but the way of the ungodly shall perish.

6
A Reason, a Warning, and an Invitation

THE LAST VERSE of Psalm 1 describes two ways: the way of the righteous and the way of the wicked. Now we see their respective ends.

A reasonable way

"The Lord knows the way of the righteous" (Psalm 1:6). He understands what the righteous need on this path, and He provides it all. From predestining and choosing in eternity past to bestowing the glory of our salvation in eternity future, God provides life, relationship, and blessing. The object of life is to connect with God forever.

An unreasonable way

The way of the wicked is to run from God and disconnect from Him. The disconnected seek the good things in this life but ignore and push away the Giver of good things. The disconnected esteem themselves beyond what is warranted and get others to agree. The disconnected are fruitless and dead while still existing. Nothing accomplished transfers to the next age. The disconnected make this present life futile and empty. This is crazy.

A warning to repent

The way of the righteous never ends, but the way of the wicked is a dead end. Verse 6 says, "The way of the ungodly shall perish." It's a warning to repent and escape the wrath that is coming against sin. At a certain point, God is going call "time." He is under no obligation to support those who reject Him.

Remember when God divided the Red Sea so His people could pass through to the other side (Exodus 14)? The Egyptian army tried to bring Israel back into slavery. They actually drove their horses and chariots into the path between two walls of water that the Lord created and sustained.

The Egyptians plunged ahead in utter presumption. They enslaved and oppressed God's chosen people. They disobeyed God's command to release them. But they expected God to keep the waters of the Red Sea parted so they could capture and enslave Israel a second time!

Now why should God hold up those waters and help out the Egyptians? What did He owe those arrogant, stubborn twerps? Not one blessed thing. He crushed the Egyptians in the collapsing waters. Their end had come.

In the same way, God is not obligated to continue holding up our world, though He does so because He is gracious and merciful. He is "not willing that any should perish but that all should come to repentance" (2 Peter 3:9). Psalm 1 and the rest of the Bible give notice to the world that wickedness will not be permitted to go on indefinitely. God will judge Satan, He will judge angels, He will judge all the world in righteousness. No one will escape judgment.

Judgment and choice

This is the judgment: if you want God, you can have Him. If you don't want God, you don't have to have Him.

Though God fills heaven and earth, there is one exception—one place where He does not dwell. Because He is not in that place, there is nothing good there. There is only condemnation, shame, and deprivation forever. Though a person may exist forever there, the Bible calls it the second death (Revelation 20:14). It is a place of supreme misery because without God there can be no satisfaction. Existence without God is not life.

Every person must choose whether to live with God or exist without Him. If you want blessing, if you want what is good, then you must choose God and His way. If you go your own way and reject Him, then you may not have any good at all. You are headed to that place where God is not, to exist without Him and without any good forever.

The greatest invitation

The question is, do you want to wait until that great judgment or do you want to do something about it now? I say right now! When you hear His voice, respond.

We then, as workers together with Him also plead with you not to receive the grace of God in vain. For He says:

"In an acceptable time I have heard you,
And in the day of salvation I have helped you."
Behold, now is the accepted time; behold, now is the day
of salvation. (2 Corinthians 6:1–2)

Beware, brethren, lest there be in any of you an evil heart
of unbelief in departing from the living God; but exhort
one another daily, while it is called "Today," lest any of
you be hardened through the deceitfulness of sin. For we
have become partakers of Christ if we hold the beginning
of our confidence steadfast to the end, while it is said:
"Today, if you will hear His voice,
Do not harden your hearts as in the rebellion."
(Hebrews 3:12–15)

"Come now, let us reason together," says the LORD:
"Though your sins are like scarlet, they shall be as white
as snow;
though they are red like crimson,
they shall become like wool." (Isaiah 1:18)

You have a choice to make. Do you want God or do you reject
Him?

I say choose life! Choose the way of the righteous and forsake
the way of the wicked. The way of the wicked is coming to an
end. Your way is coming to an end, even if you don't live to
see God end this world. The clock is ticking.

Choose Jesus and receive Him and go His way. Learn Him.
Know Him. Then you will know every blessing through con-
necting to God, the source of all blessing.

Let's pray:

Heavenly Father, I have gone my own way for too long. I have lived my life for myself. I haven't given You any thought. I haven't thanked You for all the blessings You have given me.

Now I want to go Your way. You sent Your Son Jesus to die for my sins. You raised Him from the dead, and right now He is in Your presence for me. I receive Him into my life as my Lord and Saviour. Please give me eternal life. Teach me Your ways, that I might know You. Lead me in Your everlasting way. In Jesus' name, Amen.

CONNECT

Part 2 • Application &
How to Meditate Biblically

7
Follow Him

HAVE YOU PRAYED to receive Jesus? I don't want to assume any reader of this book is already born again. I've known people who became church members without being born again. I've seen Christians so eager for others to be filled with the Holy Spirit that they don't wait to find out if they have first received Jesus.

If your foundation is wrong, your building will fall. Belonging to a church, being filled with the Spirit, and meditating are all necessary. But receiving Jesus is your foundation. I would hate for you to learn how to meditate in the Bible but miss receiving Jesus. So I invite you now to ask Jesus to come into your life.

Do you know you are a sinner? Jesus only saves people who know that they are wrong before God. He came to seek and save the lost (Luke 19:10). This is the hardest part: We think we are better than we actually are. Pray for the Holy Spirit to show you your sin.

Then turn to God. It feels like the wrong direction, doesn't it? Your sin has made God your enemy. It doesn't feel right to go to Him. You may want to run away and find a bomb shelter! But God is for you. Jesus said, "I am the way, the truth, and the life. No one comes to the Father except through Me" (John 14:6). He died as your substitute to pay the price for your sins. God placed all your offenses on Him, and He was punished in your place. He poured out His blood to redeem you. This means God bought you out of your slavery to sin through Jesus' death on the cross and His shed blood for you.

Three days later, He rose from the dead. This sign showed that Jesus' sacrifice was acceptable to God and paid the full price for every sin—past, present, and future. If Jesus hadn't paid for every sin, He would have stayed dead. His Resurrection is the sign of full forgiveness and the reality of new life.

Receive Jesus by repenting and believing. To repent means to change your mind and go in the opposite direction. Before repenting, you live for yourself. You follow the counsel of the ungodly. From now on, you will turn to the Lord Jesus. You'll see living for yourself as the wrong way. You will purpose to follow the Lord Jesus and learn of Him. Believing means you will hold what God has said about Jesus to be true.

And this is the testimony: that God has given us eternal life, and this life is in His Son. He who has the Son has life; he who does not have the Son of God does not have life. (1 John 5: 11–12)

You ask Him to come into your life and cause you to be born again.

But as many as received Him, to them He gave the right to become children of God, to those who believe in His name. (John 1: 12)

When you receive what He did for you, you also receive forgiveness. There is no more ground for Satan to accuse and condemn you. You will not go to hell when you die. You will go to heaven, where Jesus is, who is preparing a place for you even now (John 14:2).

Have you received Jesus into your life? Then follow Him with focus and force. That's our next chapter.

8

Be a Disciple

BABIES ARE GREAT. Growing up is greater. Babies grow because they eat, exercise, sleep, and learn. They are programmed to grow.

New believers in Christ are like babies. They are immature and don't know much about life in Christ, yet they have the potential to grow in knowledge, experience, and strength. Unlike babies, however, believers in Jesus don't automatically grow up. They can avoid growing spiritually. They can stay a baby as long as they want.

There is a difference between a convert and a disciple.

A convert is a beginner, someone who repents, believes the gospel, and receives Jesus as their Lord and Saviour.

A disciple is two things: (1) a learner, one who learns everything the Master teaches, and (2) a supporter, one who sticks close to their Master.

For the rest of your life, you should be a disciple. If you stop learning, you will start dying.

Jesus commanded His disciples to make disciples. Any believer can obey Him. You can start with discipling yourself— start learning Jesus' teachings and stay close to Him. All discipling that follows will come out of your own personal experience.

In Chapter 4 we looked briefly at Romans 12:1–2. Let's look at it again.

I beseech you therefore, brethren, by the mercies of God, that you present your bodies a living sacrifice, holy, acceptable to God, which is your reasonable service. And do not be conformed to this world, but be transformed by the renewing of your mind, that you may prove what is that good and acceptable and perfect will of God.
(Romans 12: 1–2)

1. Present your body

The first thing you are to do, says Paul, is present your body as a living and holy sacrifice to God (Romans 12:1). That means all of you—your past, present, future, family, possessions, time, money, job, house, car, pets, hobbies, free time, vacations—everything. Since Jesus bought you with His blood, you are His to command for His own purposes (Acts 20:28). Yield every part of your life to Him now. Whenever you find a pocket of resistance, repent and surrender it right away. Remember, you will not lose; you will only gain as you fulfill His purposes.

If you don't submit yourself, you'll end up with a divided heart, with one compartment for Jesus and one for you. This one is mine, that one is His.

That will never work, any more than you can walk to opposite sides of a room at the same time. You will either go in one direction or the other.

> **No one can serve two masters; for either he will hate the one and love the other, or else he will be loyal to the one and despise the other. You cannot serve God and mammon.** (Matthew 6:24)

2. Do not be conformed

Secondly, Paul urges you to not conform to this world. By *world*, Paul means the manner in which this fallen, sinful world thinks and acts. John explains:

> **Do not love the world or the things in the world. If anyone loves the world, the love of the Father is not in him. For all that is in the world—the lust of the flesh, the lust of the eyes, and the pride of life—is not of the Father but is of the world. And the world is passing away, and the lust of it; but he who does the will of God abides forever.** (1 John 2:15–17)

All that is in the world is lust—expecting things to satisfy us instead of God. We saw earlier that lust is the counsel of the ungodly. Lust tantalizes and promises to satisfy, but it never delivers.

It's like being adrift on the ocean in a life raft with no supplies. You get this impulse: I'm so thirsty I could drink ocean water. You know only an idiot would do that, but then you drink it anyway. It's awful and you swear you won't do that again. Then you get parched. You drink more. If you keep drinking, you'll end up dead from dehydration, with a belly full of salt water.

Lust is never fulfilled. It's not that people fail to reach their desires—they do. Businessmen become rich, protest groups change society's rules to suit them, militant terrorists achieve their goals. The antichrist will rule the world and make everyone worship him. The wicked will possess their lusts, but they won't keep them. The form of this world will pass away. All that remains will be unquenchable lust and the wrath of God forever.

You will never satisfy your desires by feeding on desires. You'll have to get off the hamster wheel of lust by thinking in a new way.

3. Be transformed

To think in a new way, your mind must be renewed (Romans 12:2). Without a new mind, you can't recognize God's good, acceptable, and perfect will. A prime example of this is the Apostle Peter.

When Jesus taught His disciples that He would suffer, be crucified, and rise on the third day, the gospel message flew right by Peter. The Messiah will die? Resurrect? What's that?

> **Then Peter took Him aside and began to rebuke Him, saying, "Far be it from You, Lord; this shall not happen to You!" But He turned and said to Peter, "Get behind Me, Satan! You are an offense to Me, for you are not mindful of the things of God, but the things of men."** (Matthew 16:22–23)

Satan is not mindful of the things of God. We may find Peter amusing, but we think the same way. The will of God comes into our lives, we see that it requires suffering, and we reject it, thinking, *That can't be right!* Then another will that's different from God's comes into our lives, and it looks like fun so we receive it. It turns out badly. We don't recognize the will of God when we see it, and we miss those good works God prepares in advance for us to walk in (Ephesians 2:10). In fact, we think no differently than an unbeliever. We easily put the necessities of life first rather than the things of God. But God wants us to break out of thinking like everyone else.

> **Therefore do not worry, saying, "What shall we eat?" or "What shall we drink?" or "What shall we wear?" For after all these things the Gentiles seek. For your heavenly Father knows that you need all these things. But seek first the kingdom of God and His righteousness, and all these things shall be added to you.** (Matthew 6:31–33)

I remember well when I had to change my thinking. The first overseas trip I took was as a musician in a Christian ministry band. My airfare was $1800. The leader of the band told us, "The band will pay for half, and each of you will pay the other half."

I thought, *Where in the world am I going to get $900? That's unfair.*

The leader went on to explain how we would get the $900: "Each of you find ten people who will commit to pray for you every day. Then tell them your needs with a newsletter. Pray in the $900."

I thought, *Oh, sure! That'll work!*

By this time, I had been a Christian for eight years, heard many Bible studies, played in a ministry band, and given up my day job to do it. I was in full-time Christian service, but I didn't believe God was going to support me. I lived with my parents, who didn't think God would support me either. They were none too excited about my course in life.

The breaking point came when I prayed—without faith—for $900. Why would God support me? I myself wouldn't support me!

But God spoke to me: *So! You're trusting Me to save your soul from hell, but you can't ask Me for $900?*

When He put it that way, it sounded ridiculous. I repented and asked Him for the $900. I can't tell exactly how it happened, but I was able to pay the bandleader $900 right when I needed to. The money wasn't the big thing. I could trust God for my needs—that was big.

I've been re-learning that lesson ever since. I think it's a cosmic joke that I am a missionary in London, England, because I'm so slow to trust Jesus and look to His ability. England is not an economically struggling country where you get a large amount of local currency per dollar. There's no bang for the buck—it's a fizzle. But God is patient with me. These days, I trust God for thousands each month.

God changed my thinking from *Can I afford it?* to *What does God want?* If He wants me to fly to Africa to teach Bible study methods, the money will be there. If I need to go to a conference in Austria, the money will be there. If my family needs something expensive, the money will be there. God convinced me that He will always provide for me to do His will.

The battle to follow Jesus is won or lost in the mind. We escape being conformed to think like the world through being transformed by the renewing of our minds.

God works in us by His Word

Notice that we don't transform ourselves. Transformation is something God does to us. Paul tells us in Romans 12 that we are to be transformed, but he doesn't indicate how it happens. That may leave us hanging, wondering how it all works.

Part of the answer is that in being born again we are given the mind of Christ (1 Corinthians 2:16). Light dawned for me when I realized that the mind of Christ is given to me so that I think the thoughts of Christ.

> **Finally, brethren, whatever things are true, whatever things are noble, whatever things are just, whatever things are pure, whatever things are lovely, whatever things are of good report, if there is any virtue and if there is anything praiseworthy—meditate on these things.** (Philippians 4:8)

This is why you meditate on the Word of God day and night. Romans 12:1–2 is the New Testament equivalent to Psalm 1. Meditation is the foundation of our discipleship with Jesus. I see no procedure or way to be transformed other than meditating in the Bible. I'm so glad meditating exists. It's wonderful to be transformed. Psalm 1 tells how to experience Romans 12:1–2.

When you put the Word of God into your heart and think deeply on it, it takes root, begins to grow, and bears fruit.

There is life and power in God's Word that transforms the way you think and live.

In a different context, Paul says, "He who sows sparingly will also reap sparingly, and he who sows bountifully will also reap bountifully" (2 Corinthians 9:6). The same principle applies here. As you plant more and more Scripture in your heart, you will bear more and more fruit.

God and the farmer have a deal

Farming involves a division of labor. It's a pact between a farmer and God. The farmer plows the soil, plants seed, clears weeds, and harvests the crop. God makes it rain and causes the crop to grow.

The farmer can't gather clouds and make it rain. God is not going to sit down on a tractor and plow. If the farmer does his job, God will do His.

It's a similar situation between God and you. You can't transform your life; that's His job. But God isn't going to plant His Word into you; that's your job.

So you have work to do, blessed work. What a glory and privilege it is to know God.

9

Begin to Meditate

W E'VE LOOKED AT reasons to meditate. Now let's do it. Consider and work through these practical issues.

1. Find a place in the Bible

How do you start meditating? Pick any book of the Bible and meditate through it from beginning to end. That way you'll get the whole message of the book.

Campbell McAlpine, in his meditation classic, *Alone with God*, says this choice comes with bad news and good news. The bad news is that you can't meditate through the whole Bible because you don't have enough time. There is more than enough to meditate on for several lifetimes. The good news is you can meditate through part of it, and those significant portions will transform you into the person God wants you to be. But how do you decide which part?

The Lord knows what you need. McAlpine says to ask the Lord. He goes on to describe four voices in your head: your own, the voice of other people, the devil's, and God's. Pray that you will be dead to yourself and what others say. The devil has nothing in you nor does he want you to meditate at all. You only want to hear the Lord's voice. Meditate on the first book that pops into your head. Start at the beginning and go verse by verse to the end.

What happened to me when I did this

I read McAlpine for the first time in the back of the band bus on a tour through the Southern United States. I asked God which book to start meditating in, but nothing came. I said, "Lord, I'm not leaving till You tell me where I'm supposed to meditate." No response. I felt like a total spiritual dud. I stayed in the back of the bus and cried and felt dumb. Then the Holy Spirit came down on me like a thick blanket of love. I knew God loved me. I still didn't know where God wanted me to begin meditating, but I knew God loved me.

Sometime later, I tried again, and this time I thought I heard, "Proverbs."

What? Oh no, not Proverbs! I thought. *Get behind me, Satan!*

I was afraid it would take me years to meditate through Proverbs. That was one reason why I quit so much in the beginning. I had to meditate through each picky little verse. It drove me crazy to go that slow. And every time I got back into meditating, I dreaded slogging through Proverbs.

I could barely meditate in the beginning. But it got easier as I kept on. Doing it over and over taught me to think and depend on the Holy Spirit for insight. Now I see how God prepared me for my life's work of teaching the Bible. He was my coach and I was working out in His gym. He trained, pushed, and strengthened me. At the time I thought it was torture. I'm okay with the result.

You don't have to immediately understand why the Lord starts you in a particular book. Take a risk and just do it.

All Scripture is given by inspiration of God, and is profitable for doctrine, for reproof, for correction, for instruction in righteousness, that the man of God may be complete, thoroughly equipped for every good work. (2 Timothy 3:16-17)

The worst case scenario is that you choose a place that isn't really speaking to you. For example, Song of Solomon. It was a favorite of the Puritans, but it may not be an ideal first choice for you. Don't feel bad. Pray for God to lead you, find another place, and start over until you find a place to meditate.

2. Study to grow from lesser to greater knowledge

One obstacle to meditating in Proverbs was figuring out what a proverb meant. Some of them are straightforward, but many are mysterious. I knew the language was English, but those words sat on the page like cold, dead lumps. They said nothing to me. I couldn't meditate on "blah, blah, blah, blah." I needed meaning. I had to learn what the proverb was saying first.

Each verse was like a walnut, with its meaning encased in hard mystery. Study cracked the mystery to get at that meaning.

Study is the art of observing closely. You pull yourself up from lesser knowledge to greater knowledge. You ask questions of the text, use dictionaries for word meanings, and search reference books for answers.

The meaning is there. Study helps you see it. I learned to study when required and then bring back what I discovered into my meditation.

My friend and yours, the dictionary

I didn't know much about how to study when I started. I improvised, trying to find a way forward in my meditation. I got tired of being stumped by words so I started looking them up in an English dictionary. When my thinking was vague, so was my understanding. Dictionary definitions were sharp and clear. Looking up words honed my understanding. When I grasped a concept, it became mine. I began to own Proverbs.

I learned to judge which shade of meaning best fit a certain context. A dictionary might give 14 definitions of a word, but the word didn't mean 14 different things at the same time. I had to plug each definition into the context to decide which one fit best. Sifting through ideas helped me think clearly.

I even began looking up words I thought I already knew. The nuances revealed patterns of meaning and jogged my memory for other scriptures that would shed light.

I recommend that you get the best dictionary possible. One is good, more is better. I have five or six on my tablet. If your favorite dictionary doesn't help with a word, maybe the others will.

Other study helps

The Complete Word Study Bible is a four-volume set that defines the Hebrew, Aramaic, and Greek words of the Bible. Plug those definitions into an English dictionary and see what you find. Similar resources are A.T. Robertson's *Word Pictures in the Greek New Testament*, Kenneth Wuest's *Word Studies* series, and *Vine's Expository Dictionary of Old and New Testament Words*. Having said that, the original language often expresses the same as the translation. Look up the word *love* in Greek and it means "love." Insightful, huh? You're back to using an English dictionary to find meaning.

The International Standard Bible Encyclopedia, or *ISBE*, is an all-purpose reference work. This work answers questions like, Who were those guys? or How long did he reign? or Where was that located? I prefer the 1978 edition over the 1917 version, even though the earlier version is cheaper. Archaeology progressed a lot in sixty years.

In the olden days before smart phones, dictionaries and reference works were tedious to use. Now you can carry huge volumes in your pocket. You can type a word and find a definition so easily that you'll do spadework quickly. There's never been a better time to study the Bible.

Is study easy? Like watching Netflix? I can't promise you that. But anything worth doing is challenging and demanding.

My son, if you receive my words,
And treasure my commands within you,
So that you incline your ear to wisdom,
And apply your heart to understanding;
Yes, if you cry out for discernment,
And lift up your voice for understanding,
If you seek her as silver,

**And search for her as for hidden treasures;
Then you will understand the fear of the LORD,
And find the knowledge of God.** (Proverbs 2:1–5)

God knows study isn't easy. But the effort is worth it when you pull silver and hidden treasures out of the dirt.

If you want to learn more about Bible study, I wrote a primer called *Handling Accurately the Word of Truth*, available on Amazon. The Holy Grail of Bible study is *Living by the Book* by Howard Hendricks and William Hendricks. Howard prepared for writing this book by teaching Bible study at Dallas Theological Seminary for over forty years. It will empower you to observe, interpret, and apply the Scriptures.

Study is not a drag when it sheds light on a verse, adds to your understanding, and feeds you with truth.

3. Write as you meditate

Writing down my thoughts as I meditate helps me grasp and understand better. Charles Spurgeon quoted M. Bautain in *Lectures to My Students*:

> **The pen is the scalpel which dissects the thoughts, and never, except when you write down what you behold internally, can you succeed in clearly discerning all that is contained in a conception, or in obtaining its well-marked scope. You then understand yourself, and make others understand you.** [1]

I use M. Bautain's scalpel and it's effective. For example, when I write out a section of the Bible, I'll notice when I write a word multiple times. Repetition is one way a writer makes their point. Find a pattern!

Sometimes I write half a thought because that's all I have. As I write, the other half of the thought shows up. Or I will write out a question to God and before I finish, I receive the answer. Interesting things happen when you write by hand. Writing my meditations also means I have them for future reference. When God shows me things in His Word, I want to hang on to them.

So I meditate by writing in a notebook. I write the date, day, and scripture so I can find it again. Then I write down dictionary definitions, other verses, and whatever I'm thinking about. I write out my prayers, my thanks, my worship, and my confessions. I go as long as I can get away with and the next day I pick up where I left off.

4. What time?

Early in the morning is good for me. Everyone else is usually in bed and it's quiet. Then I have time to burn to be with the Lord.

It's not natural for me to get up in the morning, but I do it. It's like flossing my teeth, which I'm not crazy about either. I floss because my dentist says, "Only floss the ones you want to keep." I'd much rather eat steak for the rest of my life than applesauce only, so I floss. Similarly, I meditate in the morning because it gives me something I want and need—time to know God.

Whatever time you can find to meditate, take it. Lunch break, coffee break, bus or train ride—any time can work. Be resourceful. Pray for insight. Think creatively to get that time.

5. What environment?

Someplace quiet and without distractions seems like the best option. Solitude is wonderful, but what if you can't get solitude?

My friend in ministry is an army veteran who worked with helicopters. As part of his service gear, he was issued ear defenders. Not only did they protect his ears from helicopter noise, they also helped him to read his Bible without distraction. After decades of use, they fell apart. His quiet time was not quiet until he bought new ones.

I got inspired to buy ear defenders for myself. They reduce sound by 35 decibels. Now I can have a quiet time in a coffee shop where the Muzak pounds relentlessly. I can meditate on the London Underground, on a bus, or even at a music festival. Ear defenders look unusual, which means no one will want to mess with you. So be it. I don't want you messing with me. I want to meditate.

That's one idea for making your own solitude. If it doesn't work for you, pray for insight and flexibility. God will help you find a place to meditate in peace and quiet.

6. How often do you meditate?

Psalm 1 says to meditate every day. It's not much good to eat once a month. Approach the Scriptures the same way and you'll starve spiritually. Realize you are cultivating consistency and self-discipline as well as profiting from the actual meditation. If your routine is disrupted, as happens to all of us, don't flog yourself. Just get back to it.

When I first began meditating, I used to quit frequently. It took time and growth in my determination to do it every day.

I would get convicted that I needed to get back to meditating. Start and restart if you must, and don't let the ups and downs bother you.

It's not helpful for me to stop meditating when I'm on a trip or a vacation. I like breaks from work, but I don't want a break from God. I want to stay close to Him no matter what. Meditation is my daily vacation with God.

As disciples, we're developing godly habits, and this is done privately in the presence of God while no one is looking. What we are in God's presence is the true measure of who we are, not what people think of us. So let us pursue that individual God wants us to be and nothing else.

7. How do you know you have meditated?

This is not a dumb question. Do you tingle? Do seven angels dance around your head throwing rose petals?

Meditation is a state of mind similar to prayer because you depend on the Holy Spirit as you think. It leads naturally and spontaneously to prayer. As you consider what God has said and done, you respond to Him and that is prayer. So you know you have meditated when you pray. You worship, give thanks, rejoice, or confess your sins and repent.

Here's a secret tip: If you find it tough to pray, meditate first.

8. Read to become familiar with the Bible

You greatly enhance your meditation by becoming familiar with the Bible. That's why you read—not to understand but to acquaint yourself with the text. Some people feel they have to understand every word and if they don't, they should stop until they do. It's easy to get bogged down on a question. But you need to start somewhere. Unless you read on, you will remain biblically illiterate and never get past Leviticus.

Don't worry about understanding everything. Read the Bible to know the contents of the Book, and become familiar with the questions as much as the answers. The Holy Spirit often reminds me of something I read before that sheds light on my meditating now. But if I've never read it, He can't remind me.

Read the Bible every day for the rest of your life. God will speak to you in your regular reading and show you fabulous things. You will become more and more at home in the Bible.

If you already have a plan for reading through the Bible, stick to it. If you don't have one, try this: read mornings in the New Testament and evenings in the Old Testament. This plan has the advantage of reading in both Testaments at once instead of grinding to a halt at perhaps 1 Chronicles and giving up. If one Testament isn't speaking to you, maybe the other one will. The Holy Spirit can connect something you read that morning with something you read at night or vice versa. The point is that the more familiar you are with the Bible, the better the Holy Spirit can lead you in your meditation.

You might have to play with this a bit to find the strategy that fits you. My wife found she was so tired at night that the Old Testament zonked her right to sleep. So she switched to reading the Old in the morning, when she would be fresher, and the New at night. Be flexible and explore possibilities.

How much should you read? If you read three chapters in the morning and three at night, you could read the Old Testament twice in a year and the New Testament three times.

Imagine if you did that for ten years—twenty times through the Old Testament and thirty times through the New Testament. You would be very familiar with the Bible.

A rule of thumb is to read what you can get through each day. The amount has changed for me over the years. After changing how long I pray, I couldn't fit that in with the amount I read, plus meditate. I didn't want to cut back on meditating, so I read less. I try to be flexible.

An overall grasp of Scripture is different from having a photographic memory. Some people are Bible whizzes as long as they have their own personal Bible. They can "see" the page where a certain scripture is located and they can go right to it. But when they use someone else's Bible, they are lost. They memorize a location, not a text. We want to be familiar with the text itself.

Bring variety into your reading by using different versions and translations. Paraphrases are good, like *Good News Translation*, *The New Testament in Modern English* by J.B. Phillips, or *The Living Bible*.

Make your familiarity with the Bible as complete as possible. It's not the work of a day, a month, or even a year. It's the investment of a lifetime. Believe me, it will pay off.

9. Slow is beautiful

Reading is quick. Zip through it. If God starts talking to you in your daily reading, then slow down and start receiving. When God is speaking, you listen. Meditation is slow by nature. It's not a speed sport. It takes time to consider things. Understanding can take a while. You have to be okay with how long it takes to think something through, ask for insight, and look things up. I've meditated on a verse for weeks if it's talking to me and new aspects appear. One verse might lead to another verse—or a group of verses—that start speaking to you. You might get far afield from where you began. Meditate and ponder, run your mind over the Scriptures, and think God's thoughts after Him. This will take time. It takes God six months to grow a cabbage. It takes Him a hundred years to grow an oak tree. What do you want to be, a cabbage or an oak tree?

When I accepted that meditation is naturally slow, it got easier. I didn't have the burden to make progress. My meditation time became a vacation. Vacation means getting away from the rush and stress. Imagine spending that time with One who loves you supremely. You learn how wonderful He is. You learn how wretched you are and how much more you need Him than He needs you. And then you find that He already knows this about you and loves you anyway. That's a nice break from life.

Sometimes I come away and feel like nothing happened; I can't meditate my way out of a wet paper bag. That's when I need God the most. He sustains me. I keep that appointment because I need the love of God. When He renews my life through His Word, that's the best. It's a very good way to spend time.

10. Work out your own plan

Everyone should think deeply on the Scriptures, but each one will do it uniquely. It's not a one-size-fits-all. God has a plan for you. Some need more input, some less. Comparing yourself with someone else will either make you proud or give you an inferiority complex. We measure ourselves by Christ. It keeps us humble and dependent upon Him.

NOTES

1   C. H. Spurgeon, *Lectures to My Students*, Marshall Morgan and Scott Publications, 1989, p. 141

10
Sample Meditation

IN THIS CHAPTER I'm going to think out loud so you can hear how I meditate. You'll find that you may not meditate like me. That's fine. This is like kissing your wife or husband. It's nobody's business how you do it, you just do it.

I don't meditate like Campbell McAlpine, the gentleman from whom I learned how to meditate, nor George Müller (yes, gentle reader, I've read him too). I've realized that I need to include more study in my meditation than McAlpine or Müller evidently needed. If I don't know what a verse is saying, I can't meditate on it. And so, for better or worse, this is how I do it.

Before I meditate in Psalm 103, I'll explain how we came to this place.

Slight digression—why Psalms?

I'm in the Psalms because that's where God said I should meditate. In 2007–2009 I taught a series through Psalms, which was good on one hand, but the preparation overwhelmed me. Either my usual amount of study time was not enough or I was exceedingly slow at understanding—probably both.

To make my deadlines, I meditated on the scriptures for that week in my morning quiet time. For me, that's a no-no. I usually reserve that time for my own soul's benefit, not to get work done. I know good men who do exactly the opposite so I'm not saying this is a hard-and-fast rule. My personal preference is to deliberately meditate elsewhere than the scriptures I teach on.

So for two years I would think on the week's psalms in order to teach them at the Wednesday night study. When I completed Psalms I moved on to another book of the Bible and looked forward to having "me" time again.

I asked God where in the Bible I should meditate. I had the impression that He said, "Psalms."

What? I had just meditated through Psalms. I had just taught Psalms! Really?

God didn't answer, and I thought, *Oh well. Whatever.*

I felt I knew Psalms pretty well. But with the luxury of no deadlines and quiet mornings, the Psalms humbled me. I didn't know anything; I had only scratched the surface. I had taught through Psalms blindfolded. I felt bad for those poor Wednesday night students. I got even more out of Psalm 1, and I'd been writing on it for two years. Unforgettable lesson: the Scriptures are inexhaustible.

That's why it's taken me so long to write this book. I despaired of ever getting to the bottom of Psalm 1. Finally, I decided enough was enough. Get the book out even though there's more in there. What I have is good enough for a start.

End of digression, back to meditating

I finished Psalm 102 yesterday. Today I'm beginning Psalm 103, which says it's a psalm of David.

You have to marvel at how important David is in the Bible. Moses wrote five volumes of Scripture, consisting of history, law, worship, plans for God's dwelling, and songs. After Moses, there is only a trickle of Scripture. But through David God again pours out worship, praise, lament, history, and prophecy, primarily in the form of songs.

Thank You again for David, Heavenly Father—how creative the Holy Spirit made him, and how I have learned to follow You better through his example.

> **Bless the LORD, O my soul;**
> **And all that is within me, bless His holy name!**
> **Bless the LORD, O my soul,**
> **And forget not all His benefits.** (Psalm 103:1–2)

On my tablet I look up what the word *bless* means in Hebrew (which appears three times in two verses). Spiros Zodhiates says that when a man uses *bless*, it means to worship. When God uses the word, it means to give benefits, like it says in verse 2.[1] I think, *Wow, there's a connection between God blessing me and me blessing God. He gives good things to me, and I give thanks and worship back to Him.* There is a relationship here, a connection, a bond.

Thank You, Heavenly Father, that You and I have a relationship, and we are connected by a bond.

David is talking to himself, his soul. In the *Merriam-Webster Collegiate Dictionary and Thesaurus* app on my tablet I look up the word *soul*, and it is "the immaterial part of a person, who we really are."[2] This body is temporary, but the soul is eternal.

Thank You, Heavenly Father, that I have a soul, that I exist, that I will live forever. My body is wearing out, but my soul will not wear out. Thank You.

How precious is my soul! Because I read my Bible to become familiar with it, I am reminded of what Jesus said in Matthew 16:26: "For what profit is it to a man if he gains the whole world, and loses his own soul? Or what will a man give in exchange for his soul?"

I want to keep my soul! Thank You that You made me, that I exist! Thank You for sending Jesus to save my soul! Thank You!

But David is in the body and he's telling himself to worship the Lord: "Come on, soul, get into it!" He is rousing himself, stirring himself up by way of remembrance.

Thank You that I am fearfully and wonderfully made, that I can talk to myself, exhort myself, tell myself to get with it, and do what is right. David did that, and I can do it too.

I recall what Paul said, "Therefore I remind you to stir up the gift of God which is in you through the laying on of my hands" (2 Timothy 1:6). Remembering God's gifts is good to do.

Thank You that I am being reminded to stir myself up. Do I ever stir anyone else up to remembrance? Hmmm. Help me to do that, Heavenly Father. Please give me some opportunities today. Anything You want! Here I am.

I look up the word *remember*, and it means "to bring to mind or think of again."[3] So David is thinking here, he's meditating. *Remembrance* also means "to keep in mind for attention or consideration."[4] David is giving attention to the good things God does for him. He wants to keep them in his mind. Whatever God did in the past, David wants to consider in the present. I also look up *consideration* and find it means "continuous and careful thought."[5] David is giving time, attention, and effort to think about what good things God is doing for him.

I'm so glad I have the time now to think about the Father and His goodness. Have I been giving this continuous and careful thought? Not especially.

I'm sorry I take what You do for me for granted. Please forgive me. Thank You, Heavenly Father.

David repeats, "Bless the Lord, O my soul" (Psalm 103:2). Is that too much worship? To say the same things over and over?

Because I read my Bible a lot, I think about the scene in heaven shown in Revelation 4 and 5, where angels, living creatures, and saints bow down to the Father and the Son, crying out, "Holy, holy, holy." That reminds me of Isaiah 6, where the Temple shakes as angels cry out God's holiness. What if I were in the presence of God myself? Would I be praising God like the angels? Aren't I in His presence already? He fills heaven and earth, doesn't He? He's right here in my office. Wow. Bless the Lord, O my soul—holy, holy, holy!

David tells himself to forget none of His benefits. I look up the word *benefit*, and it says, "something that produces good or helpful results or effects or that promotes well-being: advantage."[6] I look up *advantage* and find "superiority of position or condition."[7]

I think of how God promotes my well-being. He makes me superior. What am I by myself? Without benefits. Inferior. Hmm. What does *inferior* mean? I look it up: "of little or less importance, value, or merit, of low or lower degree or rank, of poor quality: mediocre."[8] I remember how "the Lord God formed man of the dust of the ground, and breathed into his nostrils the breath of life, and man became a living being" (Genesis 2:7). I know I am made of lowly dust, and I didn't even supply the dust. All that I am, all that I have, comes from my very good God. He benefits me in every way.

Without God, I am not worth very much. But with God, I am more than I could be by myself. He makes me valuable. My value doesn't come from me or anyone else; it comes from God.

Thank You for making me valuable. Thank You for giving me advantages. Thank You for promoting my well-being. Thank You that I am not on my own. Thank You for loving me.

David commands himself to not forget those benefits of God that promote his well-being. That catches my eye and I ask the text a question: Why didn't he say, "Remember"? Instead he says it negatively: "Don't forget!" Is that a warning? I look up *warning* just for kicks, and it says "to give notice to beforehand, especially of danger or evil."[9]

Is it dangerous or evil to forget the goodness of the Lord? Because I read my Bible a lot, I remember what it says in Romans 1:21: "Because, although they knew God, they did not glorify Him as God, nor were thankful, but became futile in their thoughts, and their foolish hearts were darkened."

I remember that giving thanks is the first step towards God, and unthankfulness is the first step away from Him—it's evil and dangerous. I realize one reason David practices thankfulness is to stay close to the Lord. That's safe. To be unthankful is evil and dangerous. I've read how Asaph nearly stumbled in

Psalm 73. He said, "The nearness of God is my good" (Psalm 73:28 NASB1995). Distance from God is disaster.

Do I practice thankfulness? *Some,* I lamely tell myself. *I could be safer, closer to God than I am.* Well, that's why I meditate, so I can be aware of what God is doing and give thanks more and more.

I look at my watch and realise I have to get going; I'm out of time. I'm done meditating for the day. But I have something exciting to look forward to tomorrow. I'm going to keep on looking, considering, and remembering all the good things God does for me, using Psalm 103 for a springboard.

As I go about my day, I can revisit this thought, that God gives me benefits for which I'm thankful. Can I remember all His benefits? I notice that as I give thanks, I stop worrying about my future. God has always provided for me. Is He going to abandon me now? I don't think so. Meditation makes unbelief foolish. It makes trust in God reasonable. I enjoy that.

NOTES

1. Warren Baker, Eugene E. Carpenter, Spiros Zodhiates, *Complete Word Study Bible*, AMG Publishers, for *Olive Tree Bible App*, s.v. "bless" H1288.

2. *Merriam-Webster*, s.v. "soul."

3. *Merriam-Webster*, s.v. "remember."

4 *Merriam-Webster*, s.v. "remembrance."

5. *Merriam-Webster*, s.v. "consideration."

6. *Merriam-Webster*, s.v. "benefit."

7. *Merriam-Webster*, s.v. "advantage."

8. *Merriam-Webster*, s.v. "inferior."

9. *Merriam-Webster*, s.v. "warning."

11
Make Room for the Word

A S YOU LEARN to meditate, you may notice that you enter a major conflict.

You want to obey Jesus and be His disciple. And you want to meditate in the Bible day and night. It's the foundation of your discipleship.

But the Bible does not slip gracefully and easily into your life. Reading, studying, and meditating clash with settled habits. Distractions demand your attention and bandwidth. Nature hates a vacuum. You have to fight to be in your Bible.

How do you deal with this surging current dragging you away from what you want?

To stand firm you have to decide how you will live with this holy book. You have to protect your Bible reading and meditating against thieves and destroyers who will steal them if you let them. You can't grow in your Christian life without holding to the truth. If your principles can be negotiated, they will be, and you will opt out of following Jesus every time it gets costly.

Make room in your life for the Bible. Be choosy about your input. I've learned that if I want to follow Jesus, some things don't help and I don't need them. Some are plainly the counsel of the ungodly. Psalm 1 encourages all of us to clean house.

Here are six reasons to identify and reject the stuff you don't need:

1. We can't hold on to contradictions

Merriam-Webster defines conflict as "the result of two ideas that are mutually contradicting."[1] The Word of God and the counsel of the ungodly do not belong together. In our minds they should be incompatible. You contradict yourself if you say that God's Word is true while holding on to things that deny it.

Look for God in what you listen to, read, and watch. Is it all true? Does it agree with the Bible?

At best you'll find the utter absence of God in the media. More often you'll find lies about God and blasphemy. You'll see fabrications, unreality, murders, adulteries, immoralities, stupidities. Does your media content harmonize with the Word of God?

2. We reap what we sow

What you put into your mind affects you for good or for evil.

Do not be deceived, God is not mocked; for whatever a man sows, that he will also reap. For he who sows to his

> flesh will of the flesh reap corruption, but he who sows
> to the Spirit will of the Spirit reap everlasting life.
> (Galatians 6:7–8)

We sow the things we watch, listen to, and read. It all affects us, either for good or for evil. We plant one seed and more comes up—thirty, sixty, or a hundredfold.

Input determines the output of our lives. If you put spiritual things in, out of your life will come godliness, endurance, love, and other fruits of the Spirit. If you consume fleshly things, your life will overflow with corruption.

Let's say what you plant in yourself is neither good nor bad. It's inert. It doesn't propel you to follow Jesus, and it's not super evil; it's just "bleah." You reap thirty, sixty, a hundredfold BLEAHHHHH and smother your life.

You can't sow weeds and then pray for crop failure.

Every day you put ideas, thoughts, and concepts into your life. These grow and bear fruit. Everything affects you, but you don't have to accept everything like a victim. Take control of your input.

3. To taste the sweetness

Some people coming to grips with the Bible don't have an appetite for it. It's bland compared with the entertainments they are used to. I've already spoken of this in chapter 3 (see p. 37).

The sweetness is already there in the Word of God. Ezekiel was told by God to eat His Word, a scroll written on both sides with words of lamentations, mourning, and woe. The parchment and ink weren't sweet; the subject was not sweet, but the scroll was sweet in Ezekiel's mouth (Ezekiel 2:8-3:3). The

Apostle John also ate a scroll that upset his stomach, but in his mouth it was sweet as honey (Revelation 10:8-10). Jeremiah said, "Your words were found, and I ate them, and Your word was to me the joy and rejoicing of my heart; for I am called by Your name, O LORD God of hosts" (Jeremiah 15:16).

It is sweet to hear God speaking to you, whether it is words of encouragement or words of rebuke. The Angel of the Lord commanded Hagar to return and submit herself to Sarah, words she probably didn't want to hear. But instead of complaining she marveled that God saw her and talked with her (Genesis 16:7-14). God relentlessly questioned Job till he repented in dust and ashes, but Job never complained that God spoke to him. That was the highlight of his life.

The Word of God is sweet. Doesn't it bug you that you don't taste it? That's why it's worth making room to hear the Word of God speaking to you.

> A satisfied soul loathes the honeycomb,
> But to a hungry soul every bitter thing is sweet.
> (Proverbs 27:7)

4. Only so much room

We have a limited capacity to receive input. Yet however we may differ in quantity, no one is infinite. Fill the glass up, take it to the brim, but anything poured after that spills over the top. Like it or not, this is our situation. Space is precious.

If you knew that in one hour you were going to eat a once-in-a-lifetime Christmas dinner, would you eat a bag of tortilla chips right now? Consider your bandwidth as a precious possession, not to be wasted. God gave it to you for thinking and meditating on His thoughts. What goes in first, stays. What goes in last often cannot be retained. Decide in advance what you want to retain before that bag of tortilla chips ambushes you.

5. To be significant and make a difference

This follows the last point. The writer to the Hebrews pleads with his readers to "lay aside every weight, and the sin which so easily ensnares us, and…run with endurance the race that is set before us" (Hebrews 12:1).

The laying aside of sin is obvious—why would we want to live contrary to the Lord, who bought us with His own blood? Yet laying aside every encumbrance is just as important as laying aside sin.

The ancient Greek athletes stripped all clothing away to run their fastest. Any additional weight interfered with the main thing, their running.

Weight refers to bulk, to side issues that are not the main goals of life.

Side issues are like barnacles on the hull of a ship. They are insignificant in themselves. One barnacle is not a problem. But a ship covered in barnacles is a big problem. An encrusted hull wastes energy and money, and it runs slow. Unessential things multiply like barnacles. Weights divert our energy and time away from the important things. They slow us down in our obedience to God. They are innocently dangerous.

If you give time and focus to insignificant things, you become insignificant. Your trivial life won't impel anyone to imitate you. It will be as though you never existed. That's what the devil wants for your life.

If you strip down and give yourself to significant things, your life will become bigger than just you. You will benefit lives all around you and do important things for God that last forever. That's what God wants for you.

As you live for the highest purpose, you'll benefit not only yourself but others too. They will watch how you grow and increase in Jesus and say, "Ah, that's how you do it." You'll make it easier for them to pursue Christ.

Paul exhorted Timothy, "Meditate on these things; give yourself entirely to them, that your progress may be evident to all" (1 Timothy 4:15). Timothy pursued Jesus like the leader of a jungle expedition, hacking a track through vines and undergrowth. Those who followed Timothy had an easier time walking through the jungle of discipleship. They didn't have to figure out their own way; they watched him and stuck to his effective path.

That's how Paul lived. He said, "Imitate me, just as I also imitate Christ" (1 Corinthians 11:1).

6. This is where the future is headed

In the age to come, even the bells on the horses are going to be holy to the Lord, as sacred as the crown of the high priest (Zechariah 14:20). The knowledge of the Lord will cover the earth as the waters cover the seas (Habakkuk 2:14). If God will be the focus of life then, why isn't He our focus now?

Submit to discipline

Paul didn't see Christianity as a civilian life, where he was free to make his own choices. It was a military life, where he submitted to discipline to achieve his commander's objective. Paul

116

urged Timothy to "fight the good fight of faith, lay hold on eternal life, to which you were called and have confessed the good confession in the presence of many witnesses" (1 Timothy 6:12).

You therefore must endure hardship as a good soldier of Jesus Christ. No one engaged in warfare entangles himself with the affairs of this life, that he may please him who enlisted him as a soldier. (2 Timothy 2:3–4)

A soldier can't make it alone

True confession: I have wrestled with my desires for music, art, the internet, science fiction, comic books, and even good Christian literature and commentaries. The good can be the enemy of the best. My conviction is that the Bible comes first. I want it to be the first thing I read in the morning and the last thing I read at night.

But I must fight to possess it. I, who want to meditate, can be turned around to neglect meditating. I know what I believe, but I lose strength to hold to it. Have you experienced this?

How can a weak soldier be saved? The gospel is that Jesus saves me. Anything I do now I purpose to do through Jesus, "for by strength no man shall prevail" (1 Samuel 2:9). But "I can do all things through Christ who strengthens me" (Philippians 4:13). Develop your convictions with Jesus, and depend on Him to help you hold them fast. Pursue Jesus with His help.

NOTES

1. *Merriam-Webster*, s.v. "conflict."

12
Choose This Day

DURING MY UNIVERSITY education I realized that art is really about decisions.

I make a mark on a canvas. Was that a good mark? I decide yes. Make another mark. How am I doing now? I decide good and keep going. I choose this and decide that until I finish my painting or graphic design or photograph, with all my choices considered, completed, and confirmed.

I tried to tell my daughter this when she was a kid: "Babe, art is all about decisions!" It was a little over her head. Later, when she was in university, she came to me and said, "You know, Dad, art is all about decisions." Good for her.

Art reflects life. Life is about decisions and their results. I wrote this book so that you would make a choice that has far-reaching consequences.

Choose to connect with God by meditating day and night.

When you plant an oak seed, it doesn't look like much at first. It takes twenty years to grow to maturity. You can't dig it up every five minutes to see how it's doing. You have to leave it in the ground and let it grow.

The result of your decision to plant is on the way.

In a few decades that little seed will grow up, take over the backyard, push over the fence, and break up the sidewalk. It will own the territory. Nothing can uproot it. That's the result of planting the powerful life in a seed.

Now you know that this is what God wants for you. Plant His seed in you. Be radically transformed. Grow, take over the neighbourhood, and bear lots of fruit.

You are not on your own. Do it with Him.

God bless you.

About the Author

Rob Dingman was born in Seattle, Washington, in 1957.

He was born again in 1974, when he began attending Calvary Fellowship in Seattle. There he began a lifelong involvement in the Calvary Chapel movement.

He began his ministry playing music with various Christian bands. In 1988 he and his wife Joanie spent a year playing concerts in Japan with the Robert Case Band. The following year, RCB played outreach concerts in Sweden and Poland, and they helped plant a Calvary Chapel church in Siegen, Germany.

In 1990 they left the United States for Germany to work at Calvary Chapel Siegen as missionaries. The year 1997 saw them move to England to help establish Calvary Chapel Westminster, London. Rob planted Calvary Chapel Twickenham in 2001.

He helped start other churches in Germany, Russia, and England, and has served as a board member for various English charities.

"Biblical Meditation" and "How to Study and Teach the Bible" are two favorite subjects Rob has taught in churches, conferences, and Bible colleges in Europe, Africa, and the United States.

In addition to *Connect*, Rob has written two other books, *Maintaining the Missionary Lifeline* and *Handling Accurately the Word of Truth*. All are available on Amazon.

Rob and Joanie live in London, England, and they have two daughters.

Contact Rob at https://calvarytw.uk/contact.